CityPack
Amsterdam

TERESA FISHER

Teresa Fisher is a freelance journalist who, having lived in mainland Europe for many years, remains a frequent visitor to Holland and, in particular, Amsterdam. She writes regularly for a variety of newspapers, magazines and books, including the recent AA publications CityPack Munich *and* Village France. *When Teresa is not writing she enjoys sailing and skiing.*

City-centre map continues on inside back cover ◄

AA Publishing

Contents

About this book

KEY TO SYMBOLS

✚	map reference on the fold-out map accompanying this book (see below)	🚌	nearest bus route
✉	address	⛴	nearest riverboat or ferry stop
☎	telephone number	♿	facilities for visitors with disabilities
🕐	opening hours	✋	admission charge
🍴	restaurant or café on premises or nearby	↔	other nearby places of interest
Ⓜ	nearest underground or Metro train station	❓	tours, lectures or special events
		➤	indicates the page where you will find a fuller description
🚉	nearest overground train station	ℹ	tourist information

CityPack Amsterdam is divided into six sections to cover the six most important aspects of your visit to Amsterdam. It includes:

- The author's view of the city and its people
- Itineraries, walks and excursions
- The top 25 sights to visit – as selected by the author
- Features about different aspects of the city that make it special
- Detailed listings of restaurants, hotels, shops and nightlife
- Practical information

In addition, easy-to-read side panels provide fascinating extra facts and snippets, highlights of places to visit and invaluable practical advice.

CROSS-REFERENCES

To help you make the most of your visit, cross-references, indicated by ➤, show you where to find additional information about a place or subject.

MAPS

The fold-out map in the wallet at the back of the book is a comprehensive street plan of Amsterdam. All the map references given in the book refer to this map. For example, the Westerkerk in the Westermarkt on Prinsengracht has the following information: ✚ **G5** indicating the grid square of the map in which the Westerkerk will be found.

The city-centre maps found on the inside front and back covers of the book itself are for quick reference. They show the Top 25 Sights, described on pages 24–48, plotted by number (**1** – **25**, not page number) from west to east across the city.

AREA CODE

The telephone code for Amsterdam is 020. If you call Amsterdam from outside the Netherlands, dial the country code (0031) followed by 20; to call a number in the city from elsewhere in the Netherlands, dial 020 then the subscriber number; to call a number in Amsterdam from inside the city, dial only the subscriber number.

AMSTERDAM
life

INTRODUCING AMSTERDAM

In their view

'Where else in the world are all life's commodities and all conceivable curiosities to be found as easily as here? In what other country can one find such absolute freedom?'

—René Descartes (1596–1650)

'This city seems to be double: one can also see it in the water: and the reflection of these distinguished houses in these canals makes this spot a fairyland.'

—Jean-François Regnard (1655–1709)

The Keizersgracht seen from the tower of the Westerkerk

Few cities arouse such contradictory feelings in visitors as Amsterdam: old yet modern, beautiful yet sordid, sleepy yet energetic, international in outlook yet provincial in character. One thing on which all agree, though, is that it is the most exciting, sophisticated and alluring of Dutch cities, and a place that is sure to leave a lasting impression on anyone who goes there.

Strolling along the grand horseshoe-shaped canals of the inner city, with their magnificent patrician mansions, imagine Amsterdam in its 17th-century heyday, when it became the richest city in Europe, headquarters of an empire and world capital of culture and commerce. Gentlemen's, Emperor's and Prince's Canals: their names reflect the grandeur of the Golden Age. Over five thousand of the buildings along these canals are classified monuments. At night, tiny white lights define the humpback bridges, and, as the Dutch seldom draw their curtains, you can catch glimpses of their homes at dusk – trendy warehouse conversions, perhaps, or the gilded ceilings of grand salons, all with potted plants the size of half-grown trees and bunches of fresh flowers.

Romantic, picturebook images such as these are easy to find in Amsterdam. Some people wear

clogs, cheese is sold in bright yellow rounds, the parks are ablaze with tulips in May, and windmills are on the horizon. Modern Amsterdam is not in the least quaint and timeless, though. It has many other aspects, less picturesque perhaps, but more interesting.

Historically, Amsterdam has been tolerant of minority groups, and over the centuries has provided sanctuary for victims of persecution. As a result, over a hundred different cultures, including many from the former Dutch colonies, now try to live harmoniously in this cosmopolitan city. Its tolerance has also provided the city with problems. Ever since the 1960s, when Amsterdam became the hippie capital of Europe, it has been trying to cope with 'drugs tourism'. Today its 'smoking' coffee shops, where the sale and use of soft drugs is tolerated, are the city's main attraction for many young people. The Rosse Buurt, or Red Light District, with its sleazy sexshops and barely clad prostitutes touting for business at their windows, has become a focus for criminal activity.

There is no denying, however, that the atmosphere in Holland's capital has changed over the past 25 years. The hippies, squatters and *provos* (anti-establishment rebels) of the '60s are now the conforming citizens of the '90s. The authorities are trying to play down the old capital of counter-culture image and present a more conventional view of a city where culture and fine arts – and business – flourish.

The Netherlands claims the highest concentration of museums in the world, and Amsterdam boasts some of the most famous. The Rijksmuseum, with its unrivalled collection of Dutch art and the Van Gogh Museum, are, for many, reason enough to visit the city. The top museums and galleries are clustered near the

Herring city

If there had been no herring, Amsterdam might never have come into existence. In the Middle Ages, the Dutch discovered a method of curing these fish, and they became a staple food. Herring fishermen built a dam across the river Amstel and a small fishing village developed, called Amstelledamme. Its site is now Dam, Amsterdam's main square.

Colourful cheeses are a traditional part of Dutch food

Amsterdam in winter has a special charm

Double Dutch

Double Dutch (gibberish), *going Dutch* (sharing expenses equally), *a Dutch treat* (a party or outing for which the participants pay) and *Dutch courage* (false bravery fuelled by alcohol) – the numerous, mostly derogatory 'Dutch' expressions that litter the English language emerged during the 17th century and reflect the British view of their major rivals in maritime trade at the time.

Concertgebouw, Holland's world-renowned concert hall, favoured by the finest performers of classical music. There is much more to Amsterdam than classic temples of culture: many of the city's museums are quirky and off-beat; and there's enough experimental art, music, theatre and dance to satisfy the most rigorously avant-garde.

Most of the city's cultural and historic sights are packed into a small area. The best way to see them all is to walk, or to hurtle around, in true Amsterdam style, on a bicycle. The city is crammed with tiny, quirky shops, offering everything from diamonds to Delftware and from trendy hemp clothing to haute couture. There are bars to suit all moods – dark, cosy brown cafés (traditional old bars stained with centuries of tobacco smoke); designer bars; and gin-tasting houses, called *proeflokalen*, bars attached to old gin (*jenever*) distilleries, where customers could sample before buying. Once businesses close for the day, the outgoing Amsterdammers take to the streets, walking, shopping or drinking in the pavement cafés before eating out at restaurants serving cuisine from around the world, and then moving on to nightspots that tempt even the most jaded visitor. However you choose to describe it – laid-back, paradoxical, impulsive, addictive – Amsterdam embodies modern life.

AMSTERDAM IN FIGURES

People
- Population (1998): 724,908, including 140 nationalities, 30,000 university students, around 9,000 heroin addicts, 7,000 prostitutes and 3,600 police officers
- Historical growth: 1500—9,000 inhabitants; 1550—30,000; 1650—220,000; 1900—510,000; 1963—868,000
- 8.5 million tourists visit annually

City
- Total area of city: 207 sq km
- Area of water: 20 sq km
- Number of districts: 30
- Height: 3m below sea level
- Average temperatures: January 2°C, July 17°C
- Listed buildings: 6,850
- 28 public parks; 220,000 trees; 600,000 flowering bulbs
- Bicycles: 400,000

Leisure
- 141 art galleries; 65 theatres and concert halls; 42 museums; 40 cinemas; 36 discos
- 1,400 cafés and bars; 750 restaurants; 550 coffee shops
- 10,334 shops

Canals
- 160 (75km), with 2,500 registered house-boats, 1,281 bridges, 120 waterbikes, 90 islands, and 70 glass-topped *rondvaartboten* (tour boats)
- Flushed with fresh water: four times a week
- Rubbish: 100 million litres dredged each year, including up to 10,000 bicycles

On Rembrandtplein, one of Amsterdam's 1,400 cafés

A CHRONOLOGY

13th century	Herring fishermen settle on the Amstel. A dam is built across the Amstel. In 1300 the settlement is given city status.
1345	City becomes a pilgrimage centre (▶ 40).
1421	The first of several great fires; wooden houses banned in 1669 to reduce fire risk.
1425	First horseshoe canal, the Singel, is dug.
1517	Protestant Reformation in Germany; Lutheran and Calvinist ideas take root in Amsterdam.
1519	Amsterdam becomes part of the Spanish empire and nominally Catholic.
1566	Iconoclast movement against the church.
1567–68	The Duke of Alba executes thousands of Protestants; start of the Eighty Years' War against Spanish rule.
1578	Amsterdam capitulates to William of Orange; Calvinists take power.
1595–97	First voyage by Dutch traders to Indonesia.
17th century	Dutch Golden Age; the city becomes the most important port in the world.
1602	Dutch East India Company founded (▶ 12).
1613	Work starts on the Grachtengordel (Canal Ring).
1620–37	Tulip mania (▶ 38).
1632	Rembrandt moves to Amsterdam from Leiden; dies in poverty 1669 (▶ 12).
1648	End of war with Spain, which recognises Dutch independence. Work begins on a new town hall, now the Koninklijk Paleis (▶ 36).
1652–54	First of a series of wars with Britain for maritime supremacy.

1784	British navy destroys Dutch fleet.
1806	Napoleon Bonaparte takes over republic, and establishes his brother Louis Napoleon as king.
1813	After defeat of Napoleon, Prince William VI of Orange returns from exile; crowned King William I in 1814.
1876	North Sea Canal opens: brings new prosperity.
1914–18	World War I. Netherlands neutral.
1928	Amsterdam Olympics: women athletes enter.
1940–45	German Occupation in World War II.
1942	Anne Frank's family go into hiding in a house on the Prinsengracht; betrayed by an unknown informant in August 1944 (▶ 12, 31).
1948	Karel Appel helps found the CoBrA (Copenhagen, Brussels, Amsterdam) modern art movement, laying the foundations of abstract expressionism.
1940s–50s	Holland withdraws from overseas empire.
1952	Amsterdam–Rhine Canal opens.
1960s–70s	Hippies from all over Europe flock to the city.
1964–67	Anti-Establishment riots in Amsterdam.
1973	Van Gogh Museum opens (▶ 26).
1980	Queen Beatrix crowned; city named Holland's capital.
1989	City government falls because of weak anti-vehicle laws. New laws are passed to make Amsterdam eventually free of motor traffic.
1990	Van Gogh centenary exhibition attracts 890,000 visitors.
1998–99	Redevelopment of Museumplein, with a park and lake in the square; new wing added to Van Gogh Museum, another planned for Stedelijk Museum of Modern Art (▶ 25, 26).

People & Events from History

A popular monarch

Beatrix, Queen of the Netherlands, came to the throne when her mother, Queen Juliana, abdicated on 30 April 1980. Beatrix, born in 1938, was crowned at the Nieuwe Kerk. Her great popularity is reflected in the celebrations on her official birthday (*Koninginnedag,* 30 April) – a national holiday, when the entire city becomes one massive street party with market stalls, music, dancing and drinking in the jam-packed streets.

FOUNDING OF THE NETHERLANDS

In the mid-16th century the Low Countries rebelled against the religious and political oppression of Spanish rule. The resistance was led by Prince William of Orange, better known as William the Silent. In 1578 he took control of Amsterdam in a bloodless coup. The city's Catholic magistrates and clergy were deported, and Amsterdam was declared a Calvinist city within the new Dutch Republic of 1579.

DUTCH EAST INDIA COMPANY (VOC)

In 1602 a number of Amsterdam companies joined together to create the *Verenigde Oost-Indische Compagnie* (VOC) to control Dutch trading. It soon became the world's largest trading company, enjoying tremendous prosperity in the 17th century. But a series of wars in the late 17th and early 18th centuries exhausted the country. Faced also with commercial competition from Britain and France, the VOC went into decline and in 1799 was declared bankrupt.

REMBRANDT

Rembrandt Harmenszoon van Rijn (1606–69) was the most influential Dutch artist of the 17th century. Marrying a wealthy heiress in 1634, he spent his most successful years as a painter in Amsterdam; commissions poured in from wealthy patrons, beneficiaries of Amsterdam's Golden Age. Yet changing tastes in art, plus the untimely death of his wife, Saskia, in 1642, left Rembrandt impoverished (► 28, 30, 44).

ANNE FRANK

Anne Frank (1929–45) dreamed of becoming a famous writer. In 1942, with Holland under Nazi occupation, Anne's father hid his family in a house beside the Prinsengracht. Her journal during their 25 months of confinement was to posthumously realise her youthful ambition; she died at Belsen just before the war's end. *The Diary of a Young Girl*, published 1947, is read and loved worldwide; yet it not only brings her to life as an individual, but has become a voice of the many silenced in the Holocaust (► 31).

AMSTERDAM
how to organise your time

13

ITINERARIES

These four itineraries take you to some of Amsterdam's main sights. Almost all places of interest are within walking distance of each other, and the city's layout of concentric canals and crisscrossing streets forms a grid that makes it easy to get orientated. Itinerary One is based around Dam square, with Four nearby to the west on the Canal Ring. Itinerary Two lies to the southwest of the centre, while Three takes in the east side.

ITINERARY ONE	HISTORIC CITY
Morning	Visit the Amsterdams Historisch Museum (► 35) to get an idea of the city's colourful history. Then stop at the Begijnhof (► 34), Holland's finest almshouses.
Lunch	Try Caffé Esprit (► 69) or a Dutch restaurant, such as Haesje Claes (► 62).
Afternoon	Enjoy the street entertainment between visits to the sumptuous Koninklijk Paleis (Royal Palace ► 36) and Nieuwe Kerk (► 37), both on the dam (now Dam square) that gave Amsterdam its name.
Evening	Having booked in advance, if possible, go to a classical music concert at the Concertgebouw (► 54 and 78) or Beurs van Berlage, or opera or dance at the Muziektheater (► 55, 77 and 78).
ITINERARY TWO	ART TREASURES
Morning	See part of the Rijksmuseum's immense collection (► 28) – start with the paintings of the Golden Age. Then stroll through the Vondelpark (► 24).
Lunch	Picnic in the park or head for Leidseplein (► 27) for its cafés and restaurants.
Afternoon	Return to the Museumsplein for the Van Gogh Museum (► 26), or the Stedelijk Museum (► 25) that specialises in modern art. Neither should be missed.

Malevich painting in the Stedelijk Museum

ITINERARY THREE	MARITIME HISTORY
Morning	It's easy to imagine 17th-century Amsterdam at the peak of its maritime success during an early morning stroll around the Western Islands (➤ 51). A bus ride from here (🚌 **22, 28**) takes you to the Eastern Islands and the Scheepvaart Museum (➤ 47).
Lunch	Enjoy a snack at the Scheepvaart Museum restaurant.
Afternoon	Head for the Tropenmuseum (➤ 48), which re-creates tropical scenes, or walk to the Hortus Botanicus (➤ 58), the botanical gardens beside Artis Zoo (➤ 59). Continue to the Museum Willet-Holthuysen (➤ 42), built for a wealthy Golden Age merchant.
Evening	Take a candlelit canal cruise (➤ 19) and see the Golden Age buildings and canal bridges lit up.

Clogs – popular souvenirs though no longer everyday wear

ITINERARY FOUR	SIGHTSEEING AND SHOPPING
Morning	Go early to Anne Frankhuis (➤ 31) to avoid the queues. Then climb the tower of the nearby Westerkerk (➤ 30) for its breathtaking views.
Lunch	By now, you will have earned one of the Pancake Bakery's delicious *pannekoeken* (➤ 68).
Afternoon	Explore the Grachtengordel (Canal Ring) (➤ 29, 32, 50–51), and go souvenir shopping (➤ 70–76). Don't forget the Bloemenmarkt (➤ 38) for bulbs and Stoeltie Diamonds (➤ 43).
Evening	Explore the Rosse Buurt (➤ 39).

WALKS

THE CANAL RING AND JORDAAN

After breakfast at La Ruche (►69) in De
Bijenkorf department store, leave Dam square
via Paleisstraat; continue
straight on over the scenic
Singel, Herengracht and
Keizersgracht canals; and
then turn right alongside
Prinsengracht to pass the
impressively high tower of the
Westerkerk and the nearby
Anne Frankhuis (Anne
Frank's House). Cross over
Prinsengracht and double
back on yourself for a few
yards along the west bank of
the canal until you reach the peaceful, leafy
Bloemgracht canal. Turn right here, take the
second right up Tweede Leliedwarsstraat, cross
over Egelantiersgracht, and turn right along its
shady bank and then immediately left up
Tweede Egelantiersdwarsstraat into the heart of
the bohemian Jordaan district. Take time to
soak up the atmosphere in one of its numerous
cafés and browse in its tiny designer boutiques.

*Characteristic gables
along the Singel*

THE SIGHTS

- Nieuwe Kerk (► 37)
- Koninklijk Paleis (► 36)
- Singel (► 33)
- Canal Ring (► 29, 32, 50)
- Westerkerk (► 30)
- Anne Frankhuis (► 31)
- Jordaan district (► 52)

INFORMATION

Distance 4km
Time 1–2 hours
Start/End point Dam
⊞ H5
🚋 Tram 4, 9, 14, 16, 20, 24, 25

Walk on to Lijnbaansgracht, and then turn right
on to Lindengracht, once a canal and now site of
a splendid Saturday food market, to Brouwersgracht (► 50), one of Amsterdam's most attractive canals, lined with traditional Dutch barges
and houseboats. Pause for a pre-lunch drink at
the Papeneiland brown café (reputedly Amsterdam's oldest café, ► 80) on the corner of
Prinsengracht. Cross Brouwersgracht at Herengracht and continue along Brouwersgracht to the
Singel. Cross by the sluice gates and turn right
along the eastern side of the Singel, past
Amsterdam's narrowest house façade (No. 7)
and the Poezenboot – a houseboat refuge for
stray cats. To conclude the walk, turn left
at Torenstraat, cross Spui and go along
Molensteeg. Continue across Nieuwezijds
Voorburgwal, past Nieuwe Kerk on the left and
return to Dam square, for a tasty lunch of Dutch
specialities at De Roode Leeuw (► 62).

MARKETS AND MUSEUMS

Leaving Dam square via Paleisstraat, turn left on to Nieuwezijds Voorburgwal, where a stamp and coin market is held (the Postzegelmarkt ➤ 53). About 100 yards further on the left, narrow Sint Luciensteeg leads to the Amsterdams Historisch Museum. Pass through the Schuttersgalerij (Civic Guard Gallery) into a narrow lane of whitewashed houses called Gedempte Begijnensloot. At the southern end, a stone archway on your right brings you into the calm of the leafy, cobbled, Begijnhof courtyard. A further archway leads to Spui which, with its cluster of pavement cafés, makes a good coffee stop on a sunny day. On Fridays, you will find a bustling market of antiquarian books here, and on Sundays the stalls sell paintings and prints.

Head southwest from Spui and turn left along the edge of the Singel. Cross the bridge on to Koningsplein and Amsterdam's ravishing flower market, the Bloemenmarkt. Your next landmark, the Munttoren (Mint Tower) at Muntplein, is easy to spot. Turn right along the Amstel and follow it just past the Blauwbrug (Blue Bridge). Turn right along Herengracht to make a short detour to the Willet-Holthuysen Museum, which gives a rare glimpse inside one of the canal's elegant patrician mansions. On your return, cross the bridge to reach the Waterlooplein fleamarket, a hotch-potch of stalls, some with trendy clothes and others cluttered with junk. Tucked away at the far end of the market is the Museum het Rembrandthuis (Rembrandt's House), which is not to be missed. End your walk with a drink on the terrace of Café Dantzig (➤ 68) opposite the Muziektheater (➤ 55, 77 and 78) where you can watch the barges chugging up the Amstel river.

THE SIGHTS

- Amsterdams Historisch Museum (➤ 35)
- Begijnhof (➤ 34)
- Markets (➤ 53)
- Singel (➤ 33)
- Bloemenmarkt (➤ 38)
- Munttoren (➤ 55)
- Blauwbrug (➤ 54)
- Museum Willet-Holthuysen (➤ 42)
- Museum het Rembrandthuis (➤ 44)

INFORMATION

Distance 2.5km
Time 1–2 hours
Start point Dam
🚻 H5
🚊 Tram 4, 9, 14, 16, 20, 24, 25
End point: Café Dantzig
🚻 H5
🚇 Waterlooplein

Waterlooplein fleamarket

17

EVENING STROLLS

*Red Light District signs
pull no punches*

INFORMATION

Red Light District
Distance 2.5km
Time 1 hour
Start/End point Dam
⊞ H5
▣ Tram 4, 9, 14, 16, 20, 24, 25

Squares and canals
Distance 2.5km
Time 1 hour
Start point Rembrandtplein
⊞ H5
▣ Tram 4, 9, 14, 20
End point Leidseplein
⊞ G6
▣ Tram 1, 2, 5, 6, 7, 10, 20

ROSSE BUURT (RED LIGHT DISTRICT)

From Dam square, turn up Warmoesstraat (by Hotel Krasnapolsky), the city's oldest street. After the police station, turn right down Lange Niezel and then right again at Oudezijds Voorburgwal, past the venerable Oude Kerk (➤ 40), incongruous in this seedy place. Cross the canal at Stoofstraat, then turn right on to Oudezijds Achterburgwal, pass the Hash Marihuana Hemp Museum, where you can learn everything you maybe never wanted to know about hash, marijuana and hemp. Cross the bridge and follow Oude Hoogstraat to the Pillenbrug (pill-bridge), often crowded with junkies by the drug-paraphernalia store, the Head Shop. Cross the bridge and go left (north) up Klovenierburgswal to the Waag (the old weigh-house) at Nieuwmarkt. Turn left, back to Oudezijds Achterburgwal, then right along the canal past the Tattoo Museum, devoted to the art of body illustration, and the gloomy displays of the Erotic Museum. At the canal's end, go right along Vredenburgerstraat to Zeedijk (➤ 52). Follow the road to the left back to Warmoesstraat for dinner. (➤ 93, Precautions.)

SQUARES AND CANALS

From Dam square, take Paleisstraat to Singel (➤ 33) and turn south along the canalside, passing Spui and the Flower Market (➤ 38) to Rembrandtplein. Head south across Thorbeckeplein from the neon lights and pulsating music in the cafés on Rembrandtplein, and turn left on to the silent, stately Herengracht (➤ 32). Turn right on to the Amstel for a view of the illuminated Skinny Bridge (➤ 45). The next right takes you back along Keizersgracht to the enchanting Reguliersgracht. Turn right and then left to reach Herengracht's magically lit 'Golden Bend'. Cross over Vijzelstraat, then turn left and follow Nieuwe Spiegelstraat, passing a long line of antique shops as far as Lijnbaansgracht. Turn right here and at the canal's end cut across Max Euweplein, past the glitzy Casino and along the Lido, where you will finally reach the lively Leidseplein (➤ 27).

SIGHTSEEING TOURS

ON THE WATER

Holland International ✉ Prins Hendrikkade 33a ☎ 6227788 ⊙ Year-round Cruises every 15 minutes (30 minutes in winter) in glass-topped boats, called *rondvaartboten*.

Canal Bus Tours ✉ Weteingschans 24 ☎ 6239886 There is a water-bus service around the city, and two theme tours: *Rembrandt* and *City on the Water*.

Rederij Lovers Amsterdam ✉ Prins Hendrikkade 25–27 ☎ 6222181 ⊙ Daily in summer, fewer in winter Candlelit canal cruises for romantics, with music and refreshments, as well as a commentary.

Museumboat ✉ Stationsplein 8 ☎ 6222181 Links seven jetties near the 20 major museums, so that you can combine canal cruising with museum visits. A day ticket costs f25; service runs every 30–45 minutes.

A boat tour gives a different view

ON DRY LAND

Yellow Bike Tours ✉ Nieuwezijds Kolk 29 ☎ 6206940 ⊙ Daily Apr–Oct View the city at a sedate pace or head out to the waterlands north of Amsterdam to visit windmills and a clog factory.

Tourist Tram ✉ Centraal Station ☎ 0900/9292 ⊙ Sun, in summer & holidays An hourly tram linking city sights.

Amsterdam Travel and Tours ✉ Dam 10 ☎ 6276236 ⊙ Fri 9pm Organised walking tour of the Red Light District.

Audio Tourist ✉ Oude Spiegelstraat 9 ☎ 4215580 ⊙ Apr–Sep: daily 9–6. Oct–Mar: Tue–Sun 10–5 Guide yourself around town with the help of a map and audio cassette.

FROM THE AIR

KLM Helicopter Tours ✉ Schiphol Airport ☎ 4747747 ⊙ Depends on weather Breathtaking views of the city.

Watery ways

The view of Amsterdam from the water is unforgettable. Alternatives to the glass-topped tour boats are water taxi (✉ Stationsplein 8 ☎ 6222181), or pedal boat, rented from Canal Bike (✉ Weteringschans 24 ☎ 6265574) for f12.50 per person per hour for 1–2 people; f10 for 3–4 people (with a f50 deposit).

EXCURSIONS

Haarlem
Distance 20km west
Travel time 17 minutes
🚉 Train from
   Centraal Station
✉ Stationsplein 1
☎ 0900/6161600

Keukenhof
Distance 39km southwest
Travel time 1 hour
🚉 Combined rail/bus/admission
   tickets from Centraal Station
✉ Lisse
☎ 0252/465555
🕐 End Mar–end May daily 8–6
🍴 Very expensive

Delft
Distance 50km southwest
Travel time 30 minutes
🚉 Train from Centraal Station to
   The Hague then change for
   Delft
✉ Markt 85
☎ 015/2126100

Edam
Distance 15km north
Travel time 20 minutes
🚌 Bus from Centraal Station
✉ Damplein 1
☎ 0299/315215

HAARLEM

As you wander through the historic heart of Haarlem it is hard to believe that this is the eighth largest city in Holland and the centre of Dutch printing, pharmaceutical and bulb-growing industries. The brick-paved, traffic-free streets are lined with elegant Renaissance buildings, and have hardly changed since the town's 17th-century heyday. For centuries, the town's main meeting place has been the lively main square – Grote Markt – today bordered with busy pavement cafés. The nearby Grote Kerk boasts one of the world's largest and finest organs, an ornate instrument which has drawn many renowned composers to the city, including Handel and 'Mozart. Haarlem's greatest attraction, however, is the Frans Hals Museum, home of the world's best collection of works by this painter. A short cruise can be taken along the river from the Gravenstenenbrug lift bridge.

KEUKENHOF GARDENS

These gardens at the heart of the *Bloembollenstreek* bulb-growing region rank among the most famous in the world. The site – 28ha of wooded park close to Lisse – was acquired in 1949 as a showcase. Visit between March and late May, when more than seven million bulbs are in bloom, laid out in brilliant swathes of red, yellow, pink and blue. Few people leave without a bag of bulbs for their own garden.

Keukenhof Gardens blaze with colour

DELFT

The name of this charming old town is known the world over for its blue-and-white pottery, but it was also the birthplace of the artist Johannes Vermeer (1632–75). His simple grave can be seen in the Oude Kerk along with those of other eminent Delft citizens, including Antonie van Leeuwenhoek, inventor of the microscope.

William of Orange (▶ 12) led his revolt against Spanish rule from the Prinsenhof in Delft. The building now houses the city museum, which includes a collection of rare antique Delftware. Halfway up the stairs can still be seen the holes made by the bullets that killed William in 1584. His elaborate marble tomb, designed by Hendrick de Keyser in 1614, lies in the Nieuwe Kerk.

EDAM

Famous for its ball-shaped cheeses wrapped in wax (red for export, yellow for local consumption), Edam is everyone's idea of a typical Dutch town – full of narrow, tree-shaded canals lined by gabled, red-roofed houses and crossed by wooden lift bridges. Edam enjoyed its heyday during the Golden Age, when shipbuilding, fishing and cheese brought prosperity. A traditional cheese market still takes place on Wednesday mornings in July and August. The colourful cheeses arrive by boat and are weighed

at the Kaasmarkt's 16th-century weigh-house. The method for producing long-lasting pressed cheeses was perfected in the Middle Ages, though the process is now automated. You can see it in action at three farms near Edam; leaflets are available from the tourist office (VVV) in the Town Hall.

Delftware

Delftware was developed from majolica in the 16th century by immigrant Italian potters who produced wall tiles with motifs of Dutch landscapes, animals and flowers. Over the next hundred years, trade with the East brought other influences; delicate Chinese porcelain inspired finer work. By 1652 De Porceleyne Fles was one of 32 thriving potteries here. Today it is the only original Delftware factory in production, and offers daily guided tours.

21

WHAT'S ON

Amsterdam's year is punctuated with fairs, festivals and street parties celebrating everything from cycling to Santa Claus, including the party to end all parties, the Queen's birthday. For details of events pick up a copy of the main English language listings magazine *What's On*, available from newsagents and tourist offices, or the free monthly *Amsterdam Times*, obtainable from larger hotels.

February	*Carnival*, celebrated as a preamble to Lent.
	Dockers' Strike Commemoration (25 Feb ➤ 46).
March	*Stille Omgang* (second Sun): silent procession celebrating Amsterdam's miracle (➤ 40).
April	*National Museum Weekend* (mid-month): free or reduced entrance to all museums.
	Koninginnedag (30 Apr): the Queen's birthday.
	World Press Photo Exhibition (end-Apr).
May	*Remembrance Day* (4 May): two minutes' silence at 8PM following a ceremony at Dam square in remembrance of World War II victims.
	Liberation Day (5 May): celebrations marking the end of the German Occupation in 1945.
	National Windmill Day (second Sat ➤ 60).
	National Cycling Day (second Sun).
June	*Holland Festival:* international arts festival.
	Open-air Theatre Season in Vondelpark (until mid-August ➤ 24).
	Grachtenloop canal race (second Sun): along the banks of Prinsengracht and Vijzelgracht.
July	*Summer Festival:* alternative arts festival.
August	*Dammen Op De Dam* (mid-Aug): open-air draughts tournament in Dam square.
	Prinsengracht concert (last Fri): classical music recitals on barges outside the Hotel Pulitzer.
September	*Bloemencorso* (first Sat): parade of flower-laden floats from Aalsmeer to Amsterdam.
	National Monument Day (second Sat): monuments and buildings, usually closed, are open.
	Jordaan Folk Festival (first week): music, street parties, games and eating and drinking.
October	*Antiques Fair* (last weekend): open house at the antiques shops of the Spiegelkwartier.
November	*Sinterklaas* (Santa Claus) *Parade* (➤ 57).
December	*Pakjesavond* (5 Dec): parcel evening, Holland's traditional day for present giving (➤ 57).
	Oudejaarsavond (31 Dec): New Year's Eve – wild street parties, fireworks and champagne.

AMSTERDAM's
top 25 sights

The sights are shown on the maps on the inside front cover and inside back cover, numbered **1–25** *from west to east across the city*

VONDELPARK

A favourite place for people-watching, full of joggers, sunbathers, bookworms and frisbee-throwers. Let yourself be entertained by musicians, mime artists and acrobats in this welcome splash of green near the city centre.

Open-air auditorium in Vondelpark

Pleasure gardens Amsterdam's largest and oldest municipal park – a vast 48ha rectangle of former marshland – was first opened in 1865. The designers, J D and L P Zocher, intentionally moved away from the symmetrical Dutch garden, creating in the romantic English-style with lengthy pathways, open lawns, ornamental lakes, meadows and woodland containing 120 varieties of tree, including catalpa, chestnut, cypress, oak and poplar. Financed by wealthy local residents, the Nieuwe Park (as it was then called) became the heart of a luxurious new residential district, overlooked by elegant town houses and villas. Two years later, a statue of Holland's best-known playwright, Joost van den Vondel (1587–1679) – a Dutch contemporary of Shakespeare – was erected in the park and its present name was adopted. Today, with its wide open spaces, fragrant rose garden, playgrounds, bandstand and teahouses, it remains a popular destination for family outings. It also has the Dutch Film Museum, an absolute must for cinephiles.

Like a summer-long pop festival The heyday of the always-colourful Vondelpark was in the 1970s, when hippies flocked to Amsterdam, attracted by the city's tolerance for soft drugs. Vondelpark soon became their main gathering place; the bubble burst at the end of the decade and the hippies dispersed. All that now remains are buskers, fleamarkets and the occasional ageing hippy.

STEDELIJK MUSEUM

One of the world's leading modern art museums. From Henri Matisse to Kazimir Malevich and Piet Mondrian, from Paul Klee to Vasily Kandinsky and Edward Keinholz, this gallery is an essential stop for art enthusiasts.

Controversial The Stedelijk or Municipal Museum, Amsterdam's foremost venue for contemporary art, was founded in 1895. Its collection of over 25,000 paintings, sculptures, drawings, graphics and photographs contains works by some of the great names of modern art (van Gogh, Cézanne, Picasso, Monet, Chagall), but the main emphasis is on progressive post-war movements and the exhibitions highlight the very latest, often highly controversial, trends in contemporary art. There is not enough space to keep the entire collection on view, but an extension is planned to open around 2002.

House of Museums In 1938 the Stedelijk became Holland's National Museum of Modern Art, but it achieved its worldwide avant-garde reputation in 1945–63, when it was under the dynamic direction of Willem Sandberg. He put much of its existing collection in storage and created a House of Museums in which art, photography, dance, theatre, music and cinema were all represented in innovative shows.

Cutting edge Museum highlights include suprematist paintings by Malevich; works by Mondrian, Gerrit Rietveld and other exponents of the Dutch *De Stijl* school; and a remarkable collection of almost childlike paintings by the *CoBrA* movement, founded in defiance of the artistic complacency of post-war Europe, and named after the native cities of its members – Copenhagen, Brussels and Amsterdam.

HIGHLIGHTS

- The Parakeet and the Mermaid, Matisse (1952–3)
- The Women of the Revolution, Kiefer (1986)
- My Name as Though it were Written on the Surface of the Moon, Nauman (1986)
- Sitting Woman with Fish Hat, Picasso (1942)
- The Appelbar, Appel (1951)
- Beanery, Kienholz (1965)
- Rietveld furniture collection

INFORMATION

- ✚ G6
- ✉ Paulus Potterstraat 13
- ☎ 5732911
- ◷ Daily 11–5; public hols 11–4. Closed 1 Jan
- 🍴 Restaurant (££)
- 🚊 Tram 2, 3, 5, 12, 16, 20
- ♿ Very good
- 🚻 Moderate
- ↔ Vondelpark (➤ 24), Van Gogh Museum (➤ 26), Rijksmuseum (➤ 28)
- ❓ Lectures, films and concerts. Book guided tours

Top: Special exhibitions are a feature of the Stedelijk Museum

3

VAN GOGH MUSEUM

HIGHLIGHTS

- *The Potato Eaters* (1885)
- *Self-portrait as a Painter* (1888)
- *Bedroom at Arles* (1888)
- *Vase with Sunflowers* (1888)
- *Wheatfield with Crows* (1890)

DID YOU KNOW?

- Van Gogh sold only one painting in his life time
- Record price for a van Gogh painting is f93million (1990 *Portrait of Dr Gachet*)

INFORMATION

- 🞢 G6
- ✉ Paulus Potterstraat 7
- ☎ 5705200
- 🕐 Daily 10–5. Closed 1 Jan
- 🍴 Self-service restaurant (££)
- 🚊 Tram 2, 3, 5, 12, 16, 20
- 🚢 Museumboat stop 4
- ♿ Excellent
- 💷 Expensive
- ↔ Stedelijk Museum (► 25)
  Rijksmuseum (► 28)

Top: Bedroom at Arles.
Below: a self-portrait

It is a moving experience to trace this great artist's tragic life and extraordinary achievement, through such a comprehensive display of his art, his Japanese prints and contemporary works.

World's largest van Gogh collection Of his 900 paintings and 1,200 drawings, the Van Gogh Museum has 200 and 500 respectively, together with 850 letters, Vincent's Japanese print collection, and works by friends and influential contemporaries, including Gauguin, Monet, Bernard and Pissarro. Van Gogh's paintings are arranged chronologically, starting with works from 1880 to 1887, a period characterised by realistic landscape paintings and peasant scenes in heavy tones. This period is typified by *The Potato Eaters* (1885).

Colourful palette The broad brush strokes and bold colours that characterise van Gogh's works of 1887–90 show the influence of his 1886 move to Paris and the effect of Impressionism, most striking in street and café scenes. Tired of city life, he moved in 1888 to Arles where, intoxicated by the intense sunlight and the brilliant colours of Provence, he painted many of his finest works, including *Harvest at La Crau* and the *Sunflowers* series. After snipping off a bit of his ear and offering it to a local prostitute, van Gogh voluntarily entered an asylum in St Remy, where his art took an expressionistic form. His mental anguish may be seen in the way he painted gnarled trees and menacing skies, as in the desolate *Wheatfield with Crows*. Shortly after completing it, at the age of 37, he shot himself.

New space In May 1999 the museum reopened after eight months of renovation, and construction of a new, ellipse-shaped wing designed by Japanese architect Kisho Kurokawa.

4

LEIDSEPLEIN

This square represents Amsterdam's nightlife at its vibrant best. It is filled with pavement cafés, ablaze with neon and abuzz with jugglers, buskers and fire-eaters. Be sure to spend at least one evening here.

Party centre for centuries During the Middle Ages, farmers on their way to market unloaded their carts here, at the outskirts of the city. At the turn of the century, artists and writers gathered here; in the 1930s Leidseplein was the site of many clashes between political factions, and it became the main site of anti-Nazi rallies during the war. In the 1960s it was the stomping ground of the *Pleiners* (Dutch Mods), and in 1992 it witnessed wild celebrations following local soccer team Ajax's UEFA Cup victory. Today, despite the constant flow of trams through the square, you will always find fire-eaters, sword-swallowers and other street entertainment. By night, dazzling neon lights and crowded café terraces seating over 1,000 people transform the square into an Amsterdam hot spot, busy until the early hours. Look for two notable buildings, both protected monuments: the distinctive red-brick Stadsschouwburg (Municipal Theatre), with its wide verandah and little turrets, and the art nouveau American Hotel, with its striking art deco Café Américain.

Winter wonderland Whatever the season, Leidseplein remains one of the city's main meeting places. In winter, when most tourists have returned home, it becomes quintessentially Dutch. Most of the outdoor café terraces disappear and locals huddle together for a drink and a chat in heated covered terraces, or inside the cafés. It is also *the* place to be on New Year's Eve.

HIGHLIGHTS

- American Hotel (1904)
- Stadsschouwburg (1894)
- Street entertainment

INFORMATION

- ✚ G6
- ✉ Leidseplein
- 🍴 Restaurants and cafés (£–£££)
- 🚊 Tram 1, 2, 5, 6, 7, 10, 20
- 🚢 Museumboat stop 3
- ↔ Vondelpark (▶ 24), Rijksmuseum (▶ 28), Prinsengracht (▶ 29)

Top: cafés in Leidseplein at night. Below: a stilt walker entertains

5

RIJKSMUSEUM

INFORMATION

- G6
- Stadhouderskade 42
- 6747000
- Daily 10–5. Closed 1 Jan
- Café/restaurant (££)
- Tram 2, 5, 6, 7, 10, 20
- Museumboat stop 4
- Very good
- Expensive
- Stedelijk Museum (➤ 25), Van Gogh Museum (➤ 26)
- Audio-tour

Top: The Merry Family, *Jan Steen. Below:* Self-portrait as the Apostle Paul, *Rembrandt*

Holland's biggest museum has a mind-numbing seven million items in its catalogue (not all on view), ranging from the world's most important collection of Dutch Golden Age masterpieces, through model sailing ships, to doll's houses.

Masterpieces Housed in a palatial red-brick building designed by P J H Cuypers and opened in 1885, the Rijksmuseum boasts an unrivalled collection of Old Master paintings in more than 250 rooms, a library with 250,000 volumes, a million prints and drawings, and thousands of sculptures and other artefacts. The museum's first floor traces the course of Dutch painting from religious pieces of the medieval era to the rich paintings of the Renaissance and the Golden Age, including works by Rembrandt, Vermeer, Hals and Steen. Pride of place goes to Rembrandt's *The Night Watch* (1642). This vast, dramatic canvas – one of his largest and most famous compositions, portraying a militia company – is a showpiece of 17th-century Dutch art. It was originally even bigger, but Rembrandt cut it down considerably, reputedly to get it through a doorway. Displayed in the adjacent room is a copy of *The Night Watch* attributed to Lundens, in the original form.

Treasures Along with the remarkable Dutch paintings, the museum's riches include a collection of Delftware and Meissen porcelain, countless sculptures and Asian treasures, a fascinating section on Dutch history, and two ingeniously made doll's houses – scaled-down copies of old canal houses with sumptuous 17th-century period furnishings. The refurbished south wing of the museum contains a magnificent collection of Dutch Romantic works and Impressionist paintings by local artists.

PRINSENGRACHT

Of the three canals that form the Grachtengordel (Canal Ring), Prinsengracht is in many ways the most atmospheric, with its magnificent merchants' homes, converted warehouses and flower-laden houseboats.

Prince William's canal Prinsengracht ('Prince's Canal'), named after William of Orange (▶ 12), was dug at the same time as Herengracht and Keizersgracht as part of a massive 17th-century expansion scheme. Together these three form the city's distinctive horseshoe-shaped canal network. Less exclusive than the other two waterways, with smaller houses, Prinsengracht became an important thoroughfare lined with warehouses and merchants' homes. Cargo would be unloaded from ships into fourth-storey storehouses by means of the massive hoist-beams seen today in the gables of many buildings (and still used for lifting furniture). Some houses were built with a deliberate tilt, to protect their façades from the goods as they were hoisted.

Floating homes Today, you'll also see some of Amsterdam's most beautiful houseboats moored along Prinsengracht, near Brouwersgracht and alongside the ivy-covered quays close to the Amstel. Amsterdammers have long lived in houseboats, but the housing crisis after World War II sky-rocketed the population of boat-people, so that there are more than 2,500 legal houseboats in Amsterdam, all with a postal address and mains electricity. The unofficial figure is a lot higher. You will see a variety of craft on Prinsengracht, some more seaworthy than others, ranging from solid old Rhine barges to chalet-like rafts, boats with greenhouses and gardens, and trendy studio homes.

HIGHLIGHTS

- Amstelkerk (▶ 57)
- Anne Frankhuis (▶ 31)
- Noorderkerk (▶ 57)
- Noordermarkt (▶ 53)
- Westerkerk (▶ 30)

DID YOU KNOW?

- Prinsengracht is 4.5km long, 2m deep and 25m wide to accommodate 4 lanes of shipping
- A law (dating from 1565) restricts the lean of canal houses to 1:25

INFORMATION

- ⊞ G4–G6, H6
- 🍴 Bars, cafés, restaurants (£–£££)
- 🚊 Tram 1, 2, 4, 5, 13, 14, 16, 17, 20, 24, 25
- 🚤 Museumboat stop 2
- ↔ Herengracht (▶ 32), Anne Frankhuis (▶ 31), Westerkerk (▶ 30)

WESTERKERK

- Climbing the tower
- Organ, Johannes Duyschot (1686)
- Anne Frank statue, Mari Andriessen
- Rembrandt memorial column
- Grave of Rembrandt's son, Titus

DID YOU KNOW?

- The church was consecrated in 1631
- The tower contains 48 bells
- The largest bell weighs 7,500kg and its hammer weight is 200kg

INFORMATION

- ✚ G5
- ✉ Prinsengracht 281, Westermarkt
- ☎ 6247766
- 🕓 Church mid-Apr to mid-Sep Mon–Sat 10–4; Sun 1–5. Tower Jun to mid-Sep, Wed–Sat 10–4
- 🚊 Tram 13, 14, 17, 20
- 🚤 Museumboat stop 2
- ♿ Few
- 💶 Cheap (tower)
- ↔ Prinsengracht (► 29), Anne Frankhuis (► 31)
- ❓ Carillon concerts most Tue at noon

This is the most beautiful of the four churches built in the 17th century to the north, south, east and west of the city centre. The views from the tall tower are unsurpassable.

Masterwork The West Church, the church most visited by tourists in the city, has the largest nave of any Dutch Protestant church, and the tallest tower and largest congregation in Amsterdam. It is the masterwork of Dutch architect Hendrick de Keyser, who died in 1621, one year after construction began. Designed to serve the wealthy bourgeoisie living in the smart new mansions of the Canal Ring, it was eventually completed by his son Pieter with Cornelis Dancker in 1631. To its tower they added the gaudy golden crown – a symbol of the city granted by Habsburg Emperor Maximilian 150 years earlier. The sweeping views over the Prinsengracht gables from the top of the tower, popularly called 'Lange Jan' (Tall John), make the 85m climb worthwhile. Outside the church, people often lay wreaths at the foot of the statue of Anne Frank (► 31), who used to listen to the church bells while she was in hiding, before the bells were melted down by the Nazis.

Interior The simple, whitewashed interior is laid out in the shape of a double Greek cross. The massive organ is decorated with musical instruments and frescos of the Evangelists by Gerard de Lairesse, who was one of Rembrandt's pupils. Rembrandt himself was buried here on 8 October 1669; although no trace of his pauper's grave remains, there is a memorial to him in the north aisle, near the grave of his son, Titus. The church's opening hours for visitors are not guaranteed; it may be closed at the times stated.

ANNE FRANKHUIS

"My greatest wish is to be a journalist, and later on, a famous writer...after the war, I'd like to publish a book called 'The Secret Annexe'. It remains to be seen whether I'll succeed, but my diary can serve as a basis."

Unfulfilled wish On Thursday 11 May 1944, just under three months before she was captured by the Nazis, Anne Frank wrote these poignant words in her diary. She never saw it published, but died in the concentration camp at Belsen near the end of World War II, at the age of 15.

'The Secret Annexe' After Nazi Germany invaded the Netherlands in 1940, increasingly severe anti-Semitic measures were introduced. In 1942, the Frank and van Daan families went into hiding. For the next two years, Anne Frank kept a diary describing daily life and the families' isolation and fear of discovery – until they were betrayed to the Nazis in 1944. Her father was the only member of the group to survive. In 1947, following her wishes, he published her diary, calling it *Het Achterhuis* (The Secret Annexe). Today, over half a million visitors annually make their way through the revolving bookcase that conceals the entrance into the small, gloomy rooms so vividly described in the diary. Mementoes on the walls include a map showing the Allied armies' advance from Normandy. Pencilled lines mark the children's growth. The building is preserved by the Anne Frank Foundation, an organisation founded to combat racism and anti-Semitism and to promote 'the ideals set down in the Diary of Anne Frank'. In one entry Anne wrote: 'I want to go on living even after my death!' Thanks to her diary, this wish, at least, came true.

DID YOU KNOW?

- The Nazis occupied Amsterdam for five years
- Of Holland's 140,000 pre-war Jewish population only 16,000 survived

INFORMATION

- ✚ G4
- ✉ Prinsengracht 263
- ☎ 5567100
- 🕐 Sep–Mar: daily 9–5. Apr–Aug: daily 9–9. Closed 25 Dec, 1 Jan, Yom Kippur
- 🚋 Tram 13, 14, 17, 20
- 🚤 Museumboat stop 2
- ♿ None
- 💰 Expensive
- ↔ Prinsengracht (➤ 29), Westerkerk (➤ 30)
- ❓ 5-minute introductory film

Top: the revolving bookcase. Below: sculpture of Anne Frank

HERENGRACHT

HIGHLIGHTS

- No. 43–45: oldest warehouses (1600)
- No. 54: 'House for a Prince'
- No. 168–172: Theatre Museum and Bartolotti Huis
- No. 366: Bible Museum
- No. 409–411: 'twin brothers' facing the 'twin sisters' (390–392) (matching neck-gabled houses)
- No. 475: 'Jewel of Canal Houses'
- No. 497: Kattenkabinet (cat museum)
- No. 502: House of Columns (mayor's residence)
- No. 605: Museum Willet-Holthuysen (➤ 42)

INFORMATION

- ✚ H4, H6, G4–G6
- 🍴 Bars, cafés and restaurants (£–£££)
- 🚃 Tram 1, 2, 4, 5, 13, 14, 16, 17, 20, 24, 25
- 🛥 Museumboat stop 5
- ↔ Singel (➤ 33), Museum Willet-Holthuysen (➤ 42)

Exploring the city's grandest canal is like going back through time to Amsterdam's Golden Age. These gilded houses are a case study of four centuries of Dutch architectural styles.

The Gentlemen's Canal Herengracht takes its name from the rich merchants and traders of Amsterdam's heyday, and was the first of three concentric canals dug early in the 17th century to house the city's fast-growing population. Attracting the wealthiest merchant aristocrats, it has the largest, most ostentatious houses, 400 of which are now protected monuments. The houses had to conform to many building standards. Even the colour of the front doors – 'Amsterdam green' – was regulated. Taxes were levied according to the width of the canal frontage, hence the rows of tall, narrow residences.

Gable-spotting Canal house owners expressed themselves in the elaborate decoration of their houses' gables and façades, and you can find every imaginable design along Herengracht. The earliest and most common are the *step* gable and the *spout* gable. Amsterdam's first *neck* gable (No. 168) was built in 1638 by Philip Vingboons, and the *bell* gable became popular early in the 18th century. Around this time, Louis XIV-style façades were fashionable. Number 475 is a fine example – nicknamed 'the jewel of canal houses'.

The Golden Bend Amsterdam's most extravagant mansions, with double fronts, were built between Leidsestraat and Vijzelstraat, along the stretch of the canal since dubbed the 'Golden Bend'. To this day, it remains the most prestigious address in town.

Top: a bell gable beside the Herengracht

SINGEL

On first glance, this canal looks like any other major waterway in the city. Look a little closer, though, and you will discover some of Amsterdam's most unusual and enchanting sights.

Former city 'belt' From its construction in the early 15th century until the late 16th century, the city limits were marked by the Singel (originally *Cingle*, meaning 'belt'), the city's defensive moat. Then, in 1586, the city council decided to build quays along the Singel's west bank and to convert the moat into a canal for large freight ships. Thus the Singel became the first of Amsterdam's concentric canals, and its curved shape established the horseshoe layout of the city. With the coming of the railways, canal transportation became less important and the Singel began to acquire a more residential character. Many warehouses are now converted into homes. The Nieuwe Haarlemmersluis, at the junction of Singel and Brouwersgracht, is opened nightly to top up the city's canals.

Flowers and floating felines Perhaps the most unusual house is No. 7. The narrowest house in Amsterdam, it was made no wider than a front door in order to minimise property taxes (▶32). Opposite is the *Poezenboot*, a houseboat which is a refuge for stray cats. Look out, too, for the Torensluis (Tower Lock, on the Singel's widest bridge); in the 17th century it was used as a prison. The bridge has a monument to Multatuli (1820–87), one of the Netherlands' greatest writers. Europe's only floating flower market, the Bloemenmarkt, is also on the Singel.

HIGHLIGHTS

- Poezenboot
- Bloemenmarkt (▶ 38)
- Torensluis prison cell
- Munttoren (▶ 55)
- No. 7: narrowest house façade
- No. 2, 36, 74, 83: unusual façades

INFORMATION

- ✚ H4, G5–H5
- ✉ Singel
- 🕐 Poezenboot: 1–4PM daily
- 🍴 Cafés and restaurants (£–£££)
- 🚊 Tram 13, 14, 17, 20
- ♿ Poezenboot: none
- 💶 Poezenboot: free
- ↔ Bloemenmarkt (▶ 38), Herengracht (▶ 32), Koninklijk Paleis (▶ 36), Begijnhof (▶ 34)

The Bloemenmarkt brings a riot of colour to the Singel

BEGIJNHOF

Tranquillity characterises Amsterdam's many hofjes (almshouses), none more so than this leafy oasis. The cobbled courtyard, edged with delightful buildings resembling doll's houses, looks almost like a film set.

DID YOU KNOW?

- The last Begijn died in 1971
- The Pilgrim Fathers are said to have worshipped here before crossing the Atlantic in the *Mayflower*

INFORMATION

- H5
- Gedempte Begijnsloot (entrance in Spui)
- Dawn till dusk
- Tram 1, 2, 5
- Good
- Free
- Amsterdams Historisch Museum (➤ 35), Singel (➤ 33)

Below: one of Amsterdam's oldest buildings, the Wooden House

Pious women A tiny, unlikely looking gateway leads to the Begijnhof, the oldest and finest *hofje* in the country (almshouses were charitable lodgings for the poor). This secluded community of magnificently restored old houses and gardens clustered around a small church lies a stone's throw from the main shopping thoroughfare. It was built in 1346 as a sanctuary for the *Begijnen* or Beguines, unmarried women who wanted to live in a religious community without becoming nuns. In return for modest lodging, they devoted themselves to the care of the poor and sick. Today, the Begijnhof is a residence for single women earning less than f35,000 a year, and has a five-year waiting list.

Two churches The Begijnkerk (1419), which dominates the courtyard, was confiscated from the Beguines during the Alteration in 1578 (➤ 12). The women continued to worship secretly until religious tolerance was restored over 200 years later, in 1795. Meanwhile, their precious church became a warehouse until 1607, when it was given to the Presbyterian community and renamed the Engelse Kerk (English Church). The simple interior contains pulpit panels designed by Piet Mondrian. Nearby, het Houten Huys (the Wooden House, 1477) is one of only two remaining wood-fronted houses in Amsterdam. It was built before 1521, when the use of wood as a building material was banned, following a series of fires. Look out for a nearby courtyard, with walls dotted with gable stones salvaged from demolished Begijnhof houses.

AMSTERDAMS HISTORISCH MUSEUM

Do make this excellent museum your first port of call. Once you have a grasp of Amsterdam's colourful history, walks around town are all the more rewarding.

The building This lively, informative museum traces the growth of Amsterdam from a 13th-century fishing village to bustling metropolis, through an impressive collection of paintings, maps, models and historical artefacts. They are displayed chronologically in one of the city's oldest buildings. Originally a monastery, it was occupied by the city orphanage (Burger-weeshuis) for nearly 400 years, until 1975, when it was converted into a museum. Most of the present structure dates from the 16th and 17th centuries. Throughout, you can still see evidence of its former use – notably the ceiling paintings in the Regent's Chamber and the numerous portraits of children, including Jan Carel van Speyck, who later in life became a Dutch naval hero.

The collections The first rooms of the museum chronicle the city's early history and its rise to prominence in trade and commerce. The displays include furniture, memorabilia and a map that illuminates each 25-year period of growth through the centuries. The museum's main focus is on the Golden Age and colonial expansion. Paintings and photographs illustrate the growing welfare problems of the 19th and early 20th centuries, and a small collection of relics from World War II shows how the Nazi occupation affected the city's population, ten per cent of which was Jewish. Finally, be sure not to miss the portraits of the dapper Civic Guard, an armed civilian force formed in the late 14th century to police the city, which hang in the adjoining Schuttersgalerij.

HIGHLIGHTS

- *View of Amsterdam, Cornelis Anthonisz (1538), the oldest city map*
- *The Meal of the 17 Guardsmen of Company H, Cornelis Anthonisz (1533), in the Schuttersgalerij*
- *The First Steamship on the IJ, Nicolaas Bauo (1816)*
- *Governesses at the Burgher Orphanage, Adriaen Backer (1683)*
- *Girls from the Civic Orphanage, Nicolaas van der Waay (1880)*
- *Bell room*

INFORMATION

- ✚ H5
- ✉ Kalverstraat 92, Nieuwzijds Voorburgwal 357, St Luciensteeg 27
- ☎ 5231822
- 🕐 Mon–Fri 10–5; Sat, Sun 11–5. Closed 1 Jan, 30 Apr, 25 Dec
- 🍴 David and Goliath Café (££)
- 🚊 Tram 1, 2, 4, 5, 9, 16, 20, 24, 25
- ♿ Very good
- 🚢 Museumboat stop 5
- 💰 Moderate
- 🔗 Begijnhof (▶ 34), Koninklijk Paleis (▶ 36)
- ❓ Guided tours on request: telephone in advance

Top: Armour on display in the Amsterdams Historisch Museum

KONINKLIJK PALEIS

Don't be put off by the Royal Palace's sober exterior. Stern and heavy, it belies the lavish decoration inside – a reminder of the power of Amsterdam in its heyday.

Civic pride At the height of the Golden Age, architect Jacob van Campen was commissioned to design Europe's largest and grandest town hall, and its classical design was a startling and progressive departure from the Dutch Renaissance style. The poet Constantyn Huygens called the Stadhuis 'the world's Eighth Wonder' and to this day it remains the city's only secular building on such a grand scale. Note the façade's astonishing wealth of decoration, numerous statues, an elaborate pediment and a huge cupola crowned by a galleon weather vane. During the seven years of construction, a heated argument developed as to whether a tower for the Nieuwe Kerk should have priority over a town hall. This was resolved when the old town hall burned down, and in 1655 the mayor moved into his new building.

Palatial splendour The town hall was transformed into a royal palace in 1808 after Napoleon made his brother Louis King of Holland. Today it serves as an occasional residence for Queen Beatrix, whose principal palace is in The Hague. Inside, be sure to see the Tribunal and the sumptuous Burgerzaal (Citizen's Hall), running the length of the palace, with the entire eastern and western hemispheres mapped out on the floor. The Tribunal was once the city's main courtroom, and condemned prisoners were taken from here to be hanged publicly in Dam square. The graceful Schepenzaal (Council Chamber) where the city aldermen met, has Rembrandt pupil Ferdinand Bol's painting of *Moses the Lawgiver.*

14

NIEUWE KERK

Considering its turbulent history, it is something of a miracle that Holland's magnificent national church has survived. Hearing its organ is a real treat.

Not so new The 'New' Church actually dates from the 15th century, when Amsterdam was growing at such a rate that the 'Old' Church (Oude Kerk, ➤ 40) was no longer sufficient. Construction started in 1408 but the church was several times destroyed by fire. After the Alteration in 1578, (when Amsterdam officially became Protestant), and a further fire in 1645, the church was rebuilt and reconsecrated in 1648. It has no spire: following years of fierce debate, the money designated for its construction was spent to complete the Royal Palace (➤ 36). It does have one of the finest of Amsterdam's 42 historic church organs – a Schonat-Hagerbeer organ, dating from 1650–73, with 5,005 pipes and a full-voiced sound that easily fills the church's vast interior.

Famous names At the time of the Alteration (➤ 12), Amsterdam's churches were largely stripped of their treasures, and the Nieuwe Kerk was no exception. The altar space has since been occupied by the tomb of Holland's most valiant naval hero, Admiral de Ruyter, one of many names from Dutch history, including poets P C Hooft and Joost van den Vondel, buried in the church. A window dated 1650 shows the granting of the city's coat of arms by William IV. Another, by Otto Mengelberg to mark her 40th year as queen, shows Wilhelmina at her inauguration in 1898. Dutch monarchs have been inaugurated here, from William I in 1815 to Beatrix in 1980. Although it is no longer a place of worship, it holds regular exhibitions and organ recitals.

Top: tomb of Michiel de Ruyter. Above: the Nieuwe Kerk from Dam Square

HIGHLIGHTS

- Organ, Hans Schonat and Jacob Hagerbeer (1650–73)
- Organ case, Jacob van Campen (1645)
- Pulpit, Albert Vinckenbrinck (1649)
- Tomb of Admiral de Ruyter, Rombout Verhulst (1681)

INFORMATION

- H5
- Dam
- 6268168
- Variable
- Nieuwe Café (££)
- Tram 1, 2, 4, 5, 9, 13, 14, 16, 17, 20, 24, 25
- Good
- Varies with exhibitions
- Koninklijk Paleis (➤ 36)

37

BLOEMENMARKT

Tulipa Whittalli *from Curtis's Botanical Magazine* c 1795

Golden sunflowers, deep blue irises, delicately scented roses and row upon row of tulips and brightly packaged tulip bulbs – the barges that serve as stalls for Amsterdam's fragrant flower market are ablaze with colour, whatever the season.

Floating market During the 17th and 18th centuries there were approximately 20 floating markets in Amsterdam, at least two of which gratified the Dutch passion for tulips. Nurserymen would sail up the Amstel from their smallholdings and moor here to sell their wares directly from their boats. Today, the stalls at this, the city's only remaining floating market, are permanently moored. Offering a vast variety of seasonal flowers, plants, pots, shrubs and herbs, they are supplied by the florists of Aalsmeer and the region around Haarlem (➤ 20), at the horticultural heart of Holland. With over 40,000 acres of the country devoted to bulb growing, it is easy to see why the Dutch are nicknamed 'the florists of Europe'.

Tulip mania Tulips were first spotted in Turkey by Dutch diplomats, who brought them back to Holland around 1600. Shortly afterwards, a Leiden botanist discovered ways of changing their shape and colour, and tulip cultivation rapidly became a national obsession. Prices soared, with single bulbs fetching up to f3,000 (an average worker's annual salary was f150). Some were even exchanged for houses, and an abundance of still life paintings was produced to capture prize blooms on canvas. In 1637, the bubble burst, and many people lost entire fortunes. Prices are more realistic today and tulip bulbs are popular souvenirs for tourists; the Bloemenmarkt remains the best place to buy the many varieties.

ROSSE BUURT

Amsterdam's Red Light District, bathed in a lurid red neon glow, and full of gaping tourists, junkies and pickpockets, is one of the city's greatest attractions.

Sex for sale Because of the port and its sailor population, sex is, and long has been, big business in Amsterdam. As early as the 15th century, Amsterdam was infamous as a centre of prostitution, and the lure of the Red Light District proves irresistible to most visitors to the city today. Crowds clog the narrow alleyways, sexshops, peep shows and suggestively named bars, while bored prostitutes beckon from their pink-lit windows. But there is more to the Red Light District than sex. Among the sleaziness, there are scattered some welcoming, ordinary cafés, bars and restaurants. 'Normal' people live here, too, and go about their everyday business in what, behind the tawdry façade, is an interesting part of the old city.

Drug central The Red Light District is also frequented by drug dealers, and here you will find the great majority of Amsterdam's psychedelic, marijuana-selling 'smoking' coffee shops (➤ 69). The Hash Marihuana Hemp Museum on Oudezijds Achterburgwal is the only museum in Europe tracing the history of hashish and the cannabis plant, and is next to the world's only Cannabis Connoisseurs' Club.

Precautions Watch your wallet, avoid eye contact with any undesirable characters, do not take photographs of prostitutes, and avoid poorly lit alleyways. Even though the evening is the liveliest time to visit, it is best not to wander around alone. Stay alert in the Red Light District and exercise caution in quiet areas at night, or avoid them completely.

DID YOU KNOW?

- Possession of drugs is technically illegal but the authorities tolerate possession of up to 30g of soft drugs (cannabis, hashish and marijuana) for personal use
- Drug-dealing is not allowed. 'Smoking' coffee shops are tolerated (➤ 69)
- 30 per cent of the city's hard-drug users carry the AIDS virus
- Brothels were legalised in 1990
- Half of Amsterdam's prostitutes are foreign

INFORMATION

- ✚ H4–H5
- ✉ Borders roughly denoted by Zeedijk (north), Kloveniersburgwal (east), Damstraat (south) and Warmoesstraat (west)
- 🍴 Restaurants, bars, cafés (£–£££)
- 🚇 Centraal Station, Nieuwmarkt
- 🚊 Tram 4, 9, 14, 16, 20, 24, 25
- ↔ Oude Kerk (➤ 40), Museum Amstelring (➤ 41)

OUDE KERK

HIGHLIGHTS

- Great Organ, Vatermüller
- Stained-glass windows, Lambert van Noort (1555)
- Carillon, F. Hemony (1658)

INFORMATION

- ✚ H5
- ✉ Oudekerksplein 1
- ☎ 6258284
- ⏰ Mon–Sat 11–5; Sun 1–5. Closed 1 Jan, 30 Apr
- 🚋 Tram 4, 9, 16, 20, 24, 25
- ♿ Good
- 💶 Moderate
- ↔ Rosse Buurt (➤ 39), Museum Amstelkring (➤ 41)
- ❓ Frequent organ recitals and carillon concerts

The 18th-century Great Organ

Surrounded by the cafés, bars and sex-shops, the Old Church represents an island of spirituality in the Red Light District. The contrast is typical of Amsterdam.

History Amsterdam's oldest church, dedicated to St Nicholas, the patron saint of seafarers, was built in 1306 to replace a wooden chapel that probably dated from the late 1200s. Over the centuries the church escaped the great fires that devastated so much of the city, and the imposing basilica you see today dates largely from the 14th century. Its graceful tower, added in 1565–67, contains one of the finest carillons in Holland. In the 16th century Jan Pieters Sweelinck, Holland's best-known composer, was organist here.

Miracle In the 14th century, the Oude Kerk became one of Europe's pilgrimage centres following a miracle: Communion bread regurgitated by a dying man and thrown on the fire, would not burn, and the sick man did not die. Today, thousands of Catholics still take part in the annual *Stille Omgang*, a silent nocturnal procession, but as the Oude Kerk is now Protestant, it no longer follows the ancient pilgrim route to the church, going instead to the Begijnhof.

Sober interior The stark, impressive interior has a triple nave and elaborate vaulting. Three magnificent windows in the Lady Chapel survived the Alteration, as did the finely carved choir-stools. In the 1960s some delicate 14th-century paintings were found behind layers of blue paint in the vaults. The tombstone of Rembrandt's first wife, Saskia van Uylenburg, is still in the church even though poverty drove him to sell her graveplot.

MUSEUM AMSTELKRING

Not only is this tiny museum one of the city's most surprising, it is also off the beaten tourist track, tucked away in a small, inconspicuous canal house on the edge of the Red Light District.

Best-kept secret In 1578, when the Roman Catholic city council was replaced by a Protestant one (▶ 12), Roman Catholic churches were closed throughout the city. In 1661, while Catholic church services were still forbidden, a wealthy merchant named Jan Hartman built a residence on the Oudezijds Voorburgwal, and two adjoining houses in the Heintje Hoecks-steeg. He ran a sock shop on the ground floor, lived upstairs, rented out the spare rooms in the buildings behind and cleverly converted the top two storeys of the canal house, and the attics of all three buildings, into a secret Catholic church. Religious freedom only returned with the French occupation of the Netherlands in 1795.

Hidden church This 'schuilkerk' was just one of many clandestine churches that sprang up throughout the city, but it is the only one that has been completely preserved. It was saved from demolition in 1888 by a group of historians called the Amstelkring (Amstel 'circle'), who nicknamed the church 'Our Dear Lord in the Attic'. To find a three-storey, galleried church at the top of a series of increasingly steep staircases is an awesome experience. With seating for 200 people, magnificent ecclesiastical statuary, silver, paintings, a collapsible altar and a huge organ, it is hard to believe that the services held here were really secret. Look for the resident priest's tiny hidden bedroom under the stairs, and the confessional on the landing. The rest of the complex has been restored, and provides a taste of domestic life in the 17th century.

HIGHLIGHTS

- Church of 'Our Dear Lord in the Attic'
- Altar painting *The Baptism of Christ*, Jacob de Wit (1716)
- Priest's bedroom
- Confessional
- Drawing room
- Kitchen

DID YOU KNOW?

- The altarpiece is one of three paintings by Jacob de Wit, designed to be interchangeable
- The church is still a consecrated place of worship

INFORMATION

- ✚ H4
- ✉ Oudezijds Voorburgwal 40
- ☎ 6246604
- 🕐 Mon–Sat 10–5; Sun, public hols 1–5. Closed 1 Jan, 30 Apr
- 🚉 Centraal Station
- 🚊 Tram 4, 9, 16, 20, 24, 25
- 🚉 Centraal Station
- 🚢 Museumboat stop 1
- ♿ None
- 💷 Moderate
- ↔ Rosse Buurt (▶ 39), Oude Kerk (▶ 40)
- ❓ Classical concerts during winter

Top: 'Our Dear Lord in the Attic'

41

19

MUSEUM WILLET-HOLTHUYSEN

INFORMATION

- H5–H6
- Herengracht 605
- 5231870
- Mon–Fri 10–5; Sat, Sun 11–5
- Waterlooplein
- Tram 4, 9, 14, 20
- Museumboat stop 6
- None
- Moderate
- Herengracht (► 32), Magere Brug (► 45), Joods Historisch Museum (► 46)

Behind the impressive façade of this gracious mansion lies a sumptuously furnished home with a delightful garden, a rare luxury in Amsterdam.

Insight This beautifully preserved house on Herengracht, Amsterdam's most elegant canal (► 32), was built in 1687 for Jacob Hop, a wealthy member of the city council. It changed hands many times and eventually, in 1855, came into the possession of a glass merchant named Pieter Gerard Holthuysen. On his death, it became the home of his daughter Sandra and her husband, the art-collector Abraham Willet, who together built up a valuable collection of glass, silver, ceramics and paintings. The couple bequeathed the house and its contents to the city in 1895, to be used as a museum. For many years it was visited so rarely that people joked that it was the best place for a gentleman to meet his mistress unobserved. However, following extensive restoration in 1996, the museum is attracting an increasing number of visitors, and now provides a rare insight into what life was like in the grand canal houses in the 17th to 19th centuries.

Luxury and grandeur The rooms are lavishly decorated with inlaid wood and lacquered panelling with painted ceilings. Be sure to see the Blue Room, formerly the preserve of the gentlemen of the house, and the 17th-century kitchen with its original plumbing. Guests would be entertained to tea in the tiny, round Garden Room which, painted in the customary pale green, looks out over an immaculate French-style formal garden, lined with topiary and studded with statues. This is one of the city's few surviving 18th-century gardens – and is a jewel not to be missed.

Top: the Dining Room laid ready for dinner

STOELTIE DIAMONDS

When you tour this diamond-polishing factory, be assured there is no pressure to buy, but the allure of all those dazzling jewels may well leave you mesmerised.

Diamonds are forever Amsterdam's association with diamonds dates from the 16th century, when Antwerp was taken by the Spanish and thousands of refugees fled north, including Jewish diamond cutters and the city's most prosperous Jewish merchants. Amsterdam's guild controls prevented them from entering most other trades so they soon established new businesses processing diamonds and dealing in the stones, and were thriving. By the 19th century, they were employing thousands of workers, and when vast fields of diamonds were discovered in South Africa in 1867, most of the stones were brought to Amsterdam to be cut. Amsterdam reigned as the diamond capital of the world until World War II, when most of the city's Jewish workers were deported to concentration camps. Because few returned, Antwerp regained its leadership of the world diamond market after the war, but diamonds from Amsterdam are known for their quality and outstanding workmanship.

Tour Many of Amsterdam's 24 diamond-polishing factories offer tours. Stoeltie's, which lasts about 30 minutes, includes a brief history of diamonds, their many industrial applications, how they are mined and the fine art of diamond production – a surprisingly grimy process considering the brilliant product. It is fascinating to watch the craft workers at their benches, deftly cutting, polishing, sorting and setting the glittering gems. Stoeltie Diamonds is one of five members of the Amsterdam Diamond Foundation, a symbol of quality and fair dealing, though not necessarily of modest prices.

DID YOU KNOW?

- The first records of Amsterdam's diamond industry date from 1586
- At its peak, it employed over 10,000 workers
- Only 20 per cent of diamonds are used in jewellery
- The world's largest-ever cut diamond, the Cullinan I ('Star of Africa') weighs 530 carats. The world's smallest-ever cut diamond has 57 facets and weighs 0.0012 carats. Both were processed in Amsterdam
- The General Dutch Diamond Workers Union, founded in 1894, was the first union in the world to win an eight-hour working day

INFORMATION

- ✚ H5
- ✉ Wagenstraat 13–17
- ☎ 6237601
- 🕐 Daily 9–5
- Ⓜ Waterlooplein
- 🚋 Tram 4, 9, 14, 20
- ♿ Very good
- 💲 Free
- ↔ Museum Willet-Holthuysen (➤ 42)

Top: working on diamonds

43

MUSEUM HET REMBRANDTHUIS

HIGHLIGHTS

- *Self-portrait with a Surprised Expression*
- *Jan Six*
- *Five Studies of the Head of Saskia and One of an Older Woman*
- *View of Amsterdam*
- *Christ Shown to the People*

INFORMATION

- ✚ H5
- ✉ Jodenbreestraat 4–6
- ☎ 5200400
- 🕐 Mon–Sat 10–5; Sun, public hols 1–5. Closed 1 Jan
- 🚇 Nieuwmarkt, Waterlooplein
- 🚊 Tram 9, 14, 20
- 🚢 Museumboat stop 6
- ♿ Few
- 💷 Moderate
- ↔ Joods Historisch Museum (► 46), Museum Willet-Holthuysen (► 42)
- ❓ Brief film of Rembrandt's life

Below: Self-portrait with Saskia *Rembrandt, 1636*

The absence of Rembrandt's own belongings from this intimate house is more than compensated for by its collection of his etchings, which is virtually complete. They are fascinating.

From riches to rags In this red-shuttered canal house, Rembrandt spent the happiest and most successful years of his life, producing many of his most famous paintings and prints here. Because of his wife, the wealthy heiress Saskia van Uylenburg, the up-and-coming young artist had been introduced to Amsterdam's patrician class and commissions for portraits had poured in. He had rapidly become an esteemed painter, and bought this large, three-storey house in 1639 as a symbol of his new-found respectability. After Saskia's tragic death, age 30, in 1642 shortly after the birth of their son Titus, Rembrandt's work became unfashionable, and in 1656 he was declared bankrupt. The house and most of his possessions were sold in 1658, although Rembrandt continued to live here until 1660. He died a pauper in 1669 (► 30).

Funny faces It is a strange experience to see 260 of the 280 etchings ascribed to Rembrandt in the very surroundings in which they were created. His achievements in etching were as important as those in his painting, since his mastery in this medium inspired its recognition as an art form for the first time. Four of his copper etching plates are on display on the ground floor, together with an exhibition on traditional etching techniques, and a series of biblical illustrations. Visit the first floor, too, where Rembrandt's studies of street figures are hung alongside some highly entertaining self-portraits in various guises, and some mirror-images of himself making faces.

MAGERE BRUG

This traditional double-leaf Dutch draw-bridge is a much-loved city landmark, and one of the most photographed sights in Amsterdam at night, illuminated by strings of enchanting lights.

Skinny sisters Of Amsterdam's 1,200 or so bridges, the wooden 'Skinny Bridge' is, without doubt, the best known. Situated on the Amstel river, it is a 20th-century replica of a 17th-century drawbridge. Tradition has it that, in 1670, a simple footbridge was built by two elderly sisters named *Mager* (meaning 'skinny'), who lived on one side of the Amstel and wanted easy access to their carriage and horses, stabled on the other bank. It seems more likely, however, that the bridge took its name from its narrow girth. In 1772 it was widened and became a double drawbridge, enabling ships of heavy tonnage to sail up the Amstel from the IJ, an inlet of what was then a sea called the Zuider Zee and is today the IJsselmeer, a freshwater lake.

City uproar In 1929 the city council started discussing whether to demolish the old frame, which had rotted. It was to be replaced with an electrically operated bridge. After a huge outcry, the people of Amsterdam voted overwhelmingly to save the original wooden bridge.

The present bridge, made of African azobe wood, was erected in 1969 and its mechanical drive installed in 1994. Every now and then, you can watch the bridge master raising the bridge to let boats through. He then jumps on his bicycle and rides hastily upstream to open the Amstel and Hoge sluice gates, only to mount his bike again and repeat the whole procedure.

DID YOU KNOW?

- 63,000 boats pass under the bridge each year
- Rebuilding in 1969 cost f140,000
- There are 60 drawbridges in Amsterdam

INFORMATION

- ✚ H6
- ✉ Amstel
- Ⓣ Waterlooplein
- 🚋 Tram 4, 9, 14, 20
- ℹ Museumboat stop 6
- ↔ Museum Willet-Holthuysen (➤ 42), Joods Historisch Museum (➤ 46)

Top: the Magere Brug, all lit up at night

23

JOODS HISTORISCH MUSEUM

HIGHLIGHTS

- Grote Schul (Great Synagogue, 1671)
- Holy Ark (1791)
- Haggadah Manuscript (1734)

DID YOU KNOW?

- 1597 First Jew gained Dutch citizenship
- 1602 Judaism first practised openly here
- 1671 The Grote Schul became the first synagogue in Western Europe
- 102,000 of the 140,000-strong Dutch Jewish community were exterminated in World War II
- Restoration of the synagogues cost over f13 million

INFORMATION

- H5
- Jonas Daniël Meijerplein 2–4
- 6269945
- Daily 11–5. Closed Yom Kippur
- Café (££)
- Waterlooplein
- Tram 9, 14, 20
- Museumboat stop 6
- Very good
- Moderate
- Museum het Rembrandthuis (➤ 44), Museum Willet-Holthuysen (➤ 42), Magere Brug (➤ 45)

Top: the Great Synagogue

A remarkable exhibition devoted to Judaism and the story of Jewish settlement in Amsterdam, this is of interest whether or not you're Jewish. The most memorable and poignant part portrays the horrors of the Holocaust.

Reconstruction Located in the heart of what used to be a Jewish neighbourhood, this massive complex of four synagogues forms the largest and most important Jewish museum outside Israel. The buildings lay in ruins for many years after World War II, and have only recently been painstakingly reconstructed as a monument to the strength of the Jewish faith and to the suffering of the Jewish people under the Nazis.

Historical exhibits The New Synagogue (1752) gives a lengthy, detailed history of Zionism, with displays of religious artefacts. The Great Synagogue (1671), of more general interest, defines the role of the Jewish community in Amsterdam's trade and industry. Downstairs is a chilling exhibition from the war years and a moving collection by Jewish painters, including a series entitled *Life? or Theatre?* by Charlotte Salomon, who died in Auschwitz aged 26.

The Dockworker The Nazis occupied Amsterdam in May 1940 and immediately began to persecute the Jewish population. In February 1941, 400 Jews were gathered outside the Great Synagogue by the SS, herded into trucks and taken away. This triggered the February Strike, a general strike led by dockers. Though suppressed after only two days, it was Amsterdam's first open revolt against Nazism and gave impetus to the resistance movement. Every 25 February, a ceremony at Andriessen's statue *The Dockworker* commemorates the strike.

NEDERLANDS SCHEEPVAART MUSEUM

Holland's glorious seafaring history gets due recognition at this museum, which displays with contemporary flair a superb collection of ships, full-size replicas and hundreds of models and nautical artefacts.

Admiralty storehouse The vast neoclassical building (1656) that now houses the Maritime Museum was formerly the Dutch Admiralty's central store. Here the East India Company would load their ships prior to the eight-month journey to Jakarta, headquarters of the VOC in Indonesia (▶ 12). In 1973, the arsenal was converted into this museum, which has the largest collection of ships in the world.

Voyages of discovery An ancient dug-out, a re-created section of a destroyer, schooners and luxury liners depict Holland's remarkable maritime history. Children can peer through periscopes and operate a radar set, while parents marvel at some 500 magnificent model ships and study the charts, instruments, weapons, maps and globes from the great age of exploration. Don't miss the first-ever sea atlas, the mid-16th century three-masted ship model, or the beautiful royal sloop – the 'golden coach on water' – last used in 1962 for Queen Juliana's silver wedding anniversary.

The *Amsterdam* The highlight of the museum is moored alongside – the *Amsterdam*, a replica of the 18th-century Dutch East Indiaman that sank off the English coast in 1749 during her maiden voyage. A vivid film 'Voyage to the East Indies' is shown, and in summer, actors become bawdy 'sailors', firing cannons, swabbing the decks, loading cargo and enacting burials at sea. The *Stad Amsterdam*, a replica of a clipper from 1854, began construction at the wharf in 1999.

HIGHLIGHTS

- The *Amsterdam*
- Royal sloop
- Blaeu's World Atlas (Room 1)
- First printed map of Amsterdam (Room 1)
- Three-masted ship (Room 2)
- Wartime exhibits (Rooms 21–24)

INFORMATION

- ✚ J5
- ✉ Kattenburgerplein 1
- ☎ 5232222
- 🕐 Tue–Sat 10–5; Sun & hols 12–5. (Also Mon 10–5 in summer). Closed 1 Jan. Crew on board *Amsterdam* in summer Mon–Sat 10:30–4:15; Sun 12:30–4:15. Winter Tue–Sun 11–3
- 🍴 Café (£)
- 🚌 Bus 22, 32
- 🚤 Museumboat stop 7
- ♿ Very good
- 💲 Expensive
- ↔ Artis Zoo (▶ 59), Hortus Botanicus (▶ 58)
- ❓ Souvenir and book shop, model-boat kit shop Thu and Fri only, multimedia theatre

Top: the ornate stern of the replica of the Amsterdam

47

25

TROPENMUSEUM

HIGHLIGHTS

- Bombay slums
- Arabian souk
- Bangladeshi village
- Indonesian farmhouse
- Indonesian gamelan orchestra
- Pacific carved wooden boats
- Papua New Guinean Bisj Poles
- Puppet and musical instrument collections

INFORMATION

- ✚ K6
- ✉ Linnaeusstraat 2
- ☎ 5688215. Children's Museum
  ☎ 5688233
- ◷ Mon–Fri 10–5; Sat, Sun, hols 12–5. Closed 1 Jan, 30 Apr, 5 May, 25 Dec.
  Children's Museum ◷ Wed afternoons, Sat, Sun; and Mon–Fri during school hols
- 🍴 Café and restaurant Ekeko
- 🚊 Tram 9, 14, 20
- ♿ Very good
- 💰 Expensive
- ⟷ Artis Zoo (➤ 59), Hortus Botanicus (➤ 58)
- ❓ Soeterijn Theatre. Shop
  ☎ 5688233 for further information

Top: statue of a Hindu goddess in the Tropenmuseum

In the extraordinary Tropical Museum, once a hymn to colonialism, colourful reconstructions of street scenes with sounds, photographs and slide presentations evoke contemporary life in tropical regions all over the world.

Foundations In 1859, Frederik Willem van Eeden, a member of the Dutch Society for the Promotion of Industry, was asked to establish a collection of objects from the Dutch colonies 'for the instruction and amusement of the Dutch people'. The collection started with a simple bow, arrows and quiver from Borneo and a lacquer water scoop from Palembang, then expanded at a staggering rate, as did the number of visitors. In the 1920s, to house the collection, the palatial Colonial Institute was constructed and adorned with stone friezes to reflect Holland's imperial achievements. In the 1970s, the emphasis shifted away from the glories of colonialism towards an explanation of Third World problems. Beside the museum is the Oosterpark, a pleasant green space.

Another world The precious collections are not displayed in glass cases, but instead are set out in lifelike settings, amid evocative sounds, photographs and slide presentations, so that you feel as if you've stepped into other continents. Explore a Bombay slum, feel the fabrics in an Arabian souk, have a rest in a Nigerian bar, contemplate in a Hindu temple, or listen to the sounds of Latin America in a café. There is also a theatre, the Soeterijn, where visiting performers mount performances of non-Western music, theatre and dance in the evenings. During the day, activities in the children's section, Kindermuseum TMJunior, give youngsters an insight into other cultures.

AMSTERDAM's
best

CANALS & WATERWAYS

Sunken booty

The canals receive many of the city's unwanted items. More than 100 million litres of sludge and rubbish are removed annually by a fleet of ten council boats: six for recovering floating refuse, one for retrieving bikes (about 10,000 a year), using hooks, and three dredgers. Among the 'treasures' they find are stolen wallets, parking meters, cars with failed hand brakes, and even an occasional corpse.

AMSTEL
The river is a busy commercial thoroughfare, with barges carrying goods to and from the port. Its sturdy 18th-century wooden sluice gates are closed four times a week. This enables fresh water from the IJmeer to flow into the canal network.
✚ H5–H6, H9–H10, J6–J9　🚊 Tram 4, 9, 14, 16, 20, 24, 25

AMSTERDAM–RHINE CANAL
Amsterdam's longest waterway stretches from the IJ to Switzerland.
✚ M5–M6, N6–N7　🚌 Bus 37, 220, 245

BLAUWBURGWAL
Amsterdam's shortest canal extends between Singel and Herengracht.
✚ H4　🚊 Tram 1, 2, 5, 13, 17, 20

BLOEMGRACHT AND EGELANTIERSGRACHT
These intimate, narrow thoroughfares in the Jordaan, a retreat from the hustle and bustle of the city centre, are lined with colourful small boats.
✚ G4–G5　🚊 Tram 13, 14, 17, 20

BROUWERSGRACHT
Also in the Jordaan, the Brouwersgracht owes its name to the many breweries established here in the 16th and 17th centuries. Houseboats and the old warehouses that line it (once used to store barley but today converted into luxury apartments) make this leafy canal particularly photogenic.
✚ G4–H4　🚉 Centraal Station

The junction of the Keizersgracht and the Reguliersgracht

GROENBURGWAL

This idyllic, picturesque canal near the Muziektheater was Monet's favourite.
⊞ H5 🚊 Nieuwmarkt

THE IJ

Amsterdam is situated on precariously low-lying ground at the confluence of the IJ (an inlet of the IJsselmeer lake) and the Amstel river. During Amsterdam's heyday in the 17th century, most maritime activity was centred on the IJ inlet and along Prins Hendrikkade, where the old warehouses were crammed with spices and other exotic produce from the East. Since 1876, access to the sea has been via the North Sea Canal, and the working docks are now to the west. The IJ is busy with barges sailing to and from the port, with pleasure boats, an occasional warship and cruise liner, and the free shuttle ferries to Amsterdam Noord.
⊞ F1–N6 🚊 Centraal Station

KEIZERSGRACHT

Together with Prinsengracht and Herengracht, this broad, elegant canal, built in 1612 and named Emperor's Canal after Emperor Maximilian I, completes the Grachtengordel (Canal Ring) – the trio of concentric central canals, that, intersected by a series of narrower, radial waterways, make a cobweb of water across the city.
⊞ G4–G6, H6 🚊 Tram 1, 2, 5, 13, 14, 16, 17, 20, 24, 25

LEIDSEGRACHT

One of the most exclusive addresses in town.
⊞ G5–G6 🚊 Tram 1, 2, 5

LOOIERSGRACHT

In the 17th century, the main industry in the Jordaan was tanning, hence the name Tanner's Canal. Many streets are named after the animals whose pelts were used such as Hazenstraat (Hare Street), Reestraat (Deer Street) and Wolvenstraat (Wolf Street).
⊞ G5 🚊 Tram 7, 10, 20

OUDEZIJDS ACHTERBURGWAL AND OUDEZIJDS VOORBURGWAL

In contrast to most of Amsterdam's canals, which are peaceful and romantic, parts of the Oudezijds Achterburgwal and Oudezijds Voorburgwal are lined with glaring, neon-lit bars and sexshops.
⊞ H4–H5 🚊 Tram 4, 9, 16, 20, 24, 25

REGULIERSGRACHT

Seven bridges cross the water here in quick succession. They are best viewed from the water at night, when they are lit by strings of lights.
⊞ H6 🚊 Tram 4, 16, 20, 24, 25

A bridge over the Keizersgracht

Old docklands

Amsterdam ranks among the world's 15 busiest ports, handling 45 million tonnes per year. It is Nissan's European distribution centre and the world's largest cocoa port. The city's old harbour has been taken by developers, but for a taste of its former glory, head for the Scheepvaart Museum (➤ 47) in the Eastern Islands, or to the Western Islands, where the carefully restored 17th-century warehouses, cluttered wharfs and nautical street names like Zeilmakerstraat (Sailmaker Street) and Touwslagerstraat (Rope Factory Street) offer a glimpse of old Amsterdam. (⊞ G3–H3 ✉ north of the railway between Wester-Kanal and Westerdoksdijk).

DISTRICTS

See Top 25 sights for
ROSSE BUURT (➤ 39)

A typically ornate gable

CHINATOWN
Amsterdam's 7,000-strong Chinese community earns part of its living from the numerous Chinese restaurants around Nieuwmarkt.
✚ H5   🚇 Nieuwmarkt

JODENHOEK
Jewish refugees first came here in the 16th century and settled on the cheap, marshy land southeast of Nieuwmarkt and bordered by the Amstel. Almost the entire district was razed to the ground at the end of World War II, leaving only a few synagogues (➤ 46) and diamond factories as legacy of a once-thriving community.
✚ H5, J5   🚇 Waterlooplein

DE JORDAAN
This popular bohemian quarter with its labyrinth of picturesque canals, narrow streets, trendy shops, cafés and restaurants was once a boggy meadow alongside Prinsengracht. A slum in the 17th century, it later became a more respectable working-class district. The name is believed to have come from the French *jardin*, meaning garden.
✚ G4   🚋 Tram 3, 10, 13, 14, 17, 20

Grachtengordel (Canal Ring)

The buildings along the web of canals around the medieval city centre are supported on thousands of wooden piles to stop them from sinking. Constructed as part of a massive 17th-century expansion project, the immaculate patrician mansions along Prinsengracht, Keizersgracht and Herengracht look almost like a toy town in a child's picture book, with their trim brickwork and characterful gables. The best way to enjoy their architectural details is from the water (➤ 19).

DE PIJP
This lively, multi-cultural area was once one of Amsterdam's most attractive working-class districts outside the Grachtengordel. The bustling Albert Cuypmarkt takes place daily (➤ 53), and there are several diamond-cutting workshops.
✚ H7   🚋 Tram 4, 16, 20, 24, 25

PLANTAGE
The 'Plantation' became one of Amsterdam's first suburbs in 1848. Before that, this popular and leafy residential area was parkland.
✚ J5–J6   🚋 Tram 9, 14, 20

ZEEDIJK
Once the sea wall of the early maritime settlement and until recently the haunt of sailors and shady characters, this area on the fringe of the Red Light District is home to several good bars and restaurants.
✚ H4–H5   🚇 Centraal Station   🚋 Tram 1, 2, 4, 5, 9, 13, 16, 17, 20, 24, 25

MARKETS

See Top 25 sights for
BLOEMENMARKT (▶ 38)

ALBERT CUYPMARKT
Amsterdam's best-known, cheapest general market, named after a Dutch landscape artist, attracts some 20,000 bargain hunters on busy days.
🔢 H7 ✉ Albert Cuypstraat ⏰ Mon–Sat 10–5 🚊 Tram 4, 16, 20, 24, 25

NOORDERMARKT
For a taste of the Jordaan district, head for the lively square surrounding the Noorderkerk. On Monday morning visit the *Lapjesmarkt* textile and secondhand clothing market, and on Saturday try the *Boerenmarkt* for organically grown fresh produce, crafts and birds.
🔢 G4 ✉ Noordermarkt ⏰ Mon, Sat 9–1 🚌 Bus 18, 22, 44

OUDEMANHUISPOORT
Antiquarian bookshops in an 18th-century arcade.
🔢 H5 ✉ Oudemanhuispoort ⏰ Mon–Sat 10–4 🚊 Tram 4, 9, 16, 20, 24, 25

POSTZEGELMARKT
A specialist market for stamps, coins and medals.
🔢 H4–H5 ✉ 280 Nieuwezijds Voorburgwal ⏰ Wed, Sat 1–4 🚊 Tram 1, 2, 5, 20

ROMMELMARKT
Rommel means rummaging. Bric-a-brac is your cue to the style of the place.
🔢 G5 ✉ Looiersgracht 38 ⏰ Sat–Thu 10–5 🚊 Tram 7, 10, 20

WATERLOOPLEIN FLEAMARKET
Amsterdam's liveliest market, full of funky clothes, curiosities and *junque*.
🔢 H5 ✉ Waterlooplein ⏰ Mon–Fri 9–5; Sat 8:30–5:30 Ⓜ Waterlooplein

ZWARTE MARKT
This huge indoor fleamarket outside Amsterdam (reputedly Europe's largest) has an Eastern Market overflowing with oriental merchandise.
🔢 Off map to northwest ✉ Industriegebied aan de Buitenlandenden, Beverwijk-Oost ⏰ Sat 7–5; Sun (Eastern Market only) 8–6 Ⓡ Beverwijk-Oost

Markets

Amsterdam resembles a collection of villages, each having its own local market. The daily markets at Ten Katestraat (Kinkerstraat) (🔢 F5–F6) and Dapperstraat (🔢 K6) are good for fruit and vegetables, and there is a flower market at Amstelveld (🔢 H6) every Monday morning. Sunday art markets are held at Spui from March until Christmas (🔢 G5–H5) and at Thorbeckeplein from mid-March until November (🔢 H6), while you may find a bargain at the Nieuwmarkt antiques market (🔢 H5) on Sundays in summer.

Albert Cuypmarkt

BRIDGES, BUILDINGS & MONUMENTS

Bridges

No other city in the world has so many bridges: 1,281. The majority are single or triple-arched hump-backed bridges made of brick and stone with simple cast-iron railings. The oldest bridge is the Torensluis (1648) and the best example of a traditional Dutch drawbridge is the Magere Brug (Skinny Bridge ➤ 45). The cast-iron Blauwbrug (Blue Bridge, 1874) is one of the most traditional, while the 20th-century Waals Eilandsgracht bridge, with its geometric arches, is the most modern.

99 Rokin, a modern interpretation of a canalside house

BEURS VAN BERLAGE

Designed by Hendrik Berlage and now hailed as an early modernist masterpiece, the former stock exchange provoked outrage when it opened in 1903. It is now a concert hall (➤ 78).
🔲 H4–H5 ✉ Damrak 213–279 ☎ 6268936 🕐 Daily 9–5 for exhibitions 🍴 Café Ranieri (££) 🚊 Tram 4, 9, 16, 20, 24, 25

CENTRAAL STATION

Many travellers get their first glimpse of Amsterdam's architectural wonders at P J H Cuyper's vast neoclassical station (1889), standing defiantly with its back to the River IJ.
🔲 H4 ✉ Stationsplein ☎ 0900/9292 🚇 Centraal Station

CONCERTGEBOUW

The orchestra and main concert hall of this elaborate neoclassical building have been renowned worldwide ever since the inaugural concert in 1888.
🔲 G7 ✉ Concertgebouwplein 2–6 ☎ 6718345 🕐 Box office Mon–Sat 10–7 🚊 Tram 3, 5, 12, 16, 20

ENTREPOTDOK

The old warehouses at Entrepotdok have been converted into offices and expensive apartments.
🔲 J5–L5 ✉ Entrepotdok 🚌 Bus 22

GREENPEACE HEADQUARTERS

This pragmatic city seems an appropriate home for the Greenpeace world headquarters, in a remarkable *Jugendstil* (art nouveau) building dating from 1905.
🔲 G4 ✉ Keizersgracht 174 ☎ 4223344
🚊 Tram 13, 14, 17, 20

KERWIN DUINMEYER MONUMENT

Kerwin, a 15-year-old black youth, was stabbed to death in Amsterdam in 1983. It was the first time since World War II that someone had been killed in the city because of race. His statue stands in the Vondelpark as a symbol of the Dutch fight against racism.
🔲 F6 ✉ Vondelpark (Jacob Obrechtstraat exit)
🚊 Tram 2, 3, 5, 12, 20

'T LIEVERDJE

In the '60s this little bronze statue of a boy, which

stands so innocently in the middle of the square, became a symbol of the *Provo* movement, and rallying point of frequent anti-establishment demonstrations. The name means 'Little Darling'.

G5 ✉ Spui
🚊 Tram 1, 2, 5, 20

MUNTTOREN
The tower of the former Mint was part of the southern gateway to the medieval city.

H5 ✉ Muntplein
🚊 Tram 4, 9, 14, 16, 20, 24, 25

MUZIEKTHEATER
Amsterdam's theatre for opera and dance is known locally as the 'false teeth' because of its white marble panelling and red brick roof. The complex includes the uninspiring buildings of the new town hall (Stadhuis), and the design caused great controversy when it was built in 1986, sparking riots during its construction.

H5 ✉ Waterlooplein
22 🚇 Waterlooplein

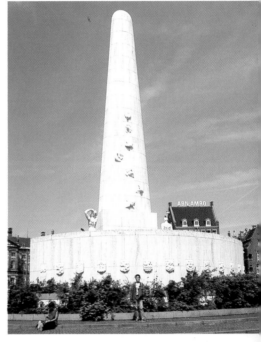

National Monument in Dam square, in memory of World War II victims

NATIONAL MONUMENT
The 75-foot obelisk in Dam square contains soil from all the Dutch provinces and former colonies. Every year on 4 May, the Queen lays a wreath here.

H5 ✉ Dam 🚊 Tram 4, 9, 14, 16, 20, 24, 25

SCHEEPVAARTHUIS
The peculiarly tapered Maritime House, encrusted with marine decoration, suggests the bow of an approaching ship. Commissioned by seven shipping companies in 1912, it represents one of the most impressive examples of the architecture of the Amsterdam School.

H5–J5 ✉ Prins Hendrikkade 108–111 🚌 Bus 22

SCHREIERSTOREN
The 'Weeping Tower' was where tearful wives and girlfriends waved farewell to their seafaring menfolk. They had good reason to weep: in the 18th century, voyages took up to four years and many sailors died.

H4 ✉ Prins Hendrikkade 94–95 🚇 Centraal Station

Homomonument
One of the city's more arresting sculptures is the *Homomonument* (1987) by Dutch artist Karin Daan, on the corner of Westermarkt and Keizersgracht. Consisting of three pink triangles, the sign homosexuals were forced to wear during the German Occupation, it commemorates all those who have been persecuted because of their homosexuality.

55

MUSEUMS & GALLERIES

Canal-house museums

The grand 17th-century canal house Museum van Loon (Keizersgracht 672) has an impressive family portrait gallery. The Theatermuseum (Herengracht 168) and the Bijbels Museum (Bible Museum) (Herengracht 366), with its religious artefacts, are also in beautiful houses whose interiors alone warrant a visit.

A mug of Heineken

Museum passes

If you intend to visit several museums and galleries, buy a *Museumjaarkaart* from the VVV (tourist office) for f17.50–f47.50 depending on age; it will give you free entry into over 400 museums throughout Holland for one year. The *Amsterdam Culture & Leisure Pass* also offers various discounts, and only costs f36.75.

HEINEKEN BROUWERIJ

Free tastings of the world's best-known brand of Dutch beer are offered at the end of a comprehensive tour of Heineken's first brewery (no longer in use).

✚ H6 ⊠ Stadhouderskade 78 ☎ 5239666 ⚙ Guided tours (18 years and over only) Mon–Fri 9:30 and 11. Also Jun to mid-Sep: 1 and 2:30. Jul and Aug: Sat 11, 1, 2:30 🚊 Tram 6, 7, 10, 16, 24, 25 ♿ Few (phone in advance) 👋 Inexpensive

MUSEUM AVIODOME

The National Aerospace Museum has aircraft from 1903 to the '90s, in addition to models of early balloons and heavier-than-air aircraft.

✚ X12 ⊠ Westelijke Randweg 201, Schiphol-Centrum ☎ 4068000 ⚙ Apr–Sep: 10–5. Oct–Mar: Tue–Fri 10–5; Sat, Sun 12–5. Closed Jan 1, Dec 25 and 31 🚉 Schiphol ♿ Good 👋 Moderate

VERZETSMUSEUM (RESISTANCE MUSEUM)

Rare wartime memorabilia and a fascinating summary of the Dutch resistance during World War II.

✚ J5 ⊠ Plantagekerklaan 61a ☎ 6202535 ⚙ Tue–Fri 10–5; Sat, Sun 1–5. Closed Jan 1, Apr 30, Dec 25 🚊 Tram 6, 9, 14, 20 ♿ Good 👋 Inexpensive

WERF 'T KROMHOUT MUSEUM

One of the city's few remaining working shipyards, this 18th-century wharf is used for restoring antique vessels, and is open to visitors during working hours.

✚ K5 ⊠ Hoogte Kadijk 147 ☎ 6276777 ⚙ Mon–Fri 10–4. Closed Sat, Sun, hols 🚌 Bus 22, 28 ♿ Few 👋 Inexpensive

WOONBOOTMUSEUM (HOUSEBOAT MUSEUM)

If you've ever wondered what life is like aboard one of Amsterdam's 2,500 houseboats, here's your chance to find out. The *Hendrika Maria*, built in 1914, was a working canal barge before being converted.

✚ G5 ⊠ By Prinsengracht 296 ☎ 4270750 ⚙ Tue–Sun 10–5. Closed Mon, public hols 🚊 Tram 1, 2, 5 ♿ None 👋 Inexpensive

PLACES OF WORSHIP

See Top 25 sights for
MUSEUM AMSTELKRING (▶ 41)
NIEUWE KERK (▶ 37)
OUDE KERK (▶ 40)
WESTERKERK (▶ 30)

AMSTELKERK
Squat and wooden, this Calvinist church (1670) was originally meant to be a temporary structure while funds were raised for a larger building elsewhere.
➕ H6 ✉ Amstelveld ☎ 6238138 🕐 Closed to public
🚋 Tram 4

FRANCISCUS XAVERIUSKERK
This splendid neo-Gothic church is often dubbed 'De Krijtberg' ('Chalk Hill'), because it is built on the site of a former chalk merchant's house.
➕ G5 ✉ Singel 442–448 ☎ 6231923 🕐 Services only
🚋 Tram 1, 2, 5, 20

NOORDERKERK
An austere church, the first in Amsterdam to be constructed in the shape of a Greek cross. It was built in 1620–23 for the Protestant workers in the Jordaan district, and is still well attended.
➕ G4 ✉ Noordermarkt 44–48 ☎ 6266436 🕐 Mon–Sat 9–6, and services 🚋 Tram 3, 10, 13, 14, 17, 20

PORTUGUESE SYNAGOGUE
Holland's finest synagogue, one of the first of any size in Western Europe. It is remarkable that this imposing building escaped destruction in World War II.
➕ J5 ✉ Mr Visserplein 3 ☎ 6245351 🕐 Sun–Fri 10–12:30, 1–4 (closes two hours before sunset on Fri). Closed Jewish holidays, Sun 10–noon 🚇 Waterlooplein 🚢 Museumboat stop 6

SINT NICOLAASKERK
Amsterdam's main Roman Catholic church (1888) and one of many Dutch churches named after St Nicholas, the patron saint of sailors. St Nicholas is also *Sinterklaas* (see panel).
➕ H4 ✉ Prins Hendrikkade 73 ☎ 6248749 🕐 Mon–Sat 11–4, and services 🚋 Tram 1, 2, 4, 5, 9, 13, 16, 17, 20, 24, 25

ZUIDERKERK
Holland's first Protestant church (1614) and indisputably one of the city's most beautiful. Its designer, Hendrick de Keyser, lies buried within. The distinctive 80m-high tower affords spectacular views of the Nieuwmarkt district.
➕ H5 ✉ Zuiderkerkhof 72 ☎ 6222962 🕐 Mon–Wed, Fri 12–5; Thu 12–8 🚇 Nieuwmarkt

Zuiderkerk

Sinterklaas

St Nicholas, or *Sinterklaas*, pays an early visit to the city each year on the third Saturday of November. Accompanied by *Zwarte Piet* (Black Peter), he arrives by boat near Sint Nicolaaskerk and distributes gingerbread to children, then receives the keys to the city from the mayor on Dam square. On 5 December (*Sinterklaasavond* or *Pakjesavond*) he comes during the night with sacks of presents for the sleeping children.

57

PARKS & GARDENS

See Top 25 sights for
OOSTERPARK, TROPENMUSEUM (► 48)
VONDELPARK (► 24)

Hortus Botanicus

Laid out in 1682, the botanical gardens were originally sponsored by the VOC (► 12), whose members brought back plants and seeds from all corners of the earth, to be grown and studied by doctors and apothecaries here. One such plant – a coffee tree – given to Louis XIV of France and cultivated in his American colonies, was the ancestor of the Brazilian coffee plantations. Likewise, the production of palm oil in Indonesia is due to plants initially cultivated here.

Vondelpark

AMSTELPARK

A formal rose garden and a rhododendron valley are two of the seasonal spectacles at this magnificent park, created in 1972 for an international horticultural exhibition. It also offers pony rides, miniature golf, a children's farm, the Rieker windmill (► 60) and other attractions. There is a special walk for blind people, and in summer you can tour the park in a miniature train.

➕ H9–H10 ◷ Dawn–dusk 🍴 Restaurant and café (££)
🚌 Bus 69, 148, 169

AMSTERDAMSE BOS

Amsterdam's largest park was built on the polders in the 1930s as part of a job creation scheme. It is a favourite family destination on weekends whatever the season – in winter, there is tobogganing and skating; in summer swimming, sailing and biking. A leisurely tram ride can be taken through the park in colourful antique cars acquired from various European cities.

➕ C10–E10 ◷ Always open 🍴 Open-air pancake restaurant and café (££) 🚌 Bus 170, 171, 172

HORTUS BOTANICUS

With more than 8,000 plant species, Amsterdam's oldest botanical garden boasts one of the largest collections in the world. It has spectacular tropical greenhouses, a medicinal herb garden, and a monumental cycad that, at 400 years old, is reputed to be the world's oldest potted plant.

➕ J5 ✉ Plantage Middenlaan 2a
☎ 6258411 ◷ Apr–Sep: Mon–Fri 9–5; Sat, Sun 11–5. Oct–Mar: Mon–Fri 9–4; Sat, Sun 11–4 🍴 Café (£)
🚊 Tram 7, 9, 14, 20 ♿ Good
Ⓜ Moderate

SARPHATIPARK

Enjoy a picnic bought at nearby Albert Cuypmarkt (► 53) in this tiny green oasis dedicated to the 19th-century Jewish doctor and city benefactor, Samuel Sarphati.

➕ H7 ◷ 9–dusk 🚊 Tram 3, 4, 16, 20, 24, 25

AMSTERDAM FOR CHILDREN

> **See Top 25 sights for:**
> **ANNE FRANKHUIS (► 31)**
> **NEDERLANDS SCHEEPVAART MUSEUM (► 47)**
> **TROPENMUSEUM (► 48)**
> **VONDELPARK (► 24)**

ARTIS ZOO (NATURA ARTIS MAGISTRA)
As well as animals, the complex includes museums, an aquarium and the Planetarium (hourly shows).
✚ J5–J6 ✉ Plantage Kerklaan 38–40 ☎ 5233400 🕐 Daily 9–5 🍴 Restaurant and café 🚊 Tram 7, 9, 14, 20. Artis Express boat from Centraal Station 🅰 Good 💲 Very expensive

CIRCUS ELLEBOOG
Learn tightrope walking, juggling and other circus skills at the Elleboog Circus. You need to book.
✚ G5 ✉ Passeerdersgracht 32 ☎ 6269370 🕐 Mon–Fri 10–5; Sat 1:30–5; Sun 10:30–4 🚊 Tram 7, 10, 20 🅰 Good 💲 Moderate

DE KRAKELING THEATER
Mime and puppet shows, for under-12s and over-12s.
✚ G5 ✉ Nieuwe Passeerderstraat 1 ☎ 6253284 🕐 Shows Mon–Fri 11–4; Sat, Sun 2–4 🚊 Tram 7, 10, 20 🅰 Good 💲 Moderate

KINDERKOOKKAFÉ
A children's restaurant where children between five and twelve can cook, then serve or eat at mini-tables.
✚ H5 ✉ Oudezijds Achterburgwal 193 ☎ 6253257 🕐 Sat cooking 3:30–6, dinner 6–8 (age 8 plus). Sun cooking 2:30–5, high tea 5–6 (age 5 plus). Mon–Fri 1–3 🚊 Nieuwmarkt 💲 Very inexpensive

KINDERBOERDERIJ DE PIJP
A 'children's farm' at the heart of the city.
✚ H7 ✉ Lizzy Ansinghstraat 82 ☎ 6648303 🕐 Wed–Mon 1–5 🚊 Tram 24, 25 🅰 Few 💲 Inexpensive

MADAME TUSSAUD SCENERAMA
Wax models of Rembrandt, Pavarotti, Schwarzenegger and other characters from the 17th century to the present day, and an amazing 5m giant clothed in windmills and tulips.
✚ H5 ✉ Dam 20 ☎ 6229949 🕐 Sep–Jun: 10–5:30. Jul–Aug: 9:30–5:30 🚊 Tram 4, 9, 14, 16, 20, 24, 25 🅰 Good 💲 Very expensive

NEWMETROPOLIS
Children will enjoy learning at this impressive new hands-on, interactive museum of modern technology.
✚ J5 ✉ Oosterdok 2 ☎ 0900/9191100 🕐 Sep–Jun: Mon–Thu 10–6; Fri–Sun 10–9. Jul–Aug: 10–9 🍴 Café 🚌 Bus 22, 32 🅰 Very good 💲 Very expensive

Out of town
Ask the VVV for details on making excursions to Volendam, where villagers still wear traditional costume; the windmill village of Zaanse Schans; to Zuiderzee, for the reconstructed fishing village of Enkhuizen; or to one of Holland's many theme parks, such as the enchanted forest of De Efteling at Kaatsheuvel or the Duinrell water park at Wassenaar, near The Hague.

Punch & Judy
From mid-April until the end of September there are free Punch and Judy performances on Wed 1–5 in Dam square.

Owl statue at the zoo

WINDMILLS

Amsterdam's most central windmill has been converted into a bar

D'ADMIRAAL
Built in 1792 to grind chalk but now unused.
✚ K1 ✉ Noordhollandsch Kanaaldijk, near Jan Thoméepad
🚌 Bus 34, 37, 39, 242

ERIJ 't IJ

DE BLOEM
This old grain mill, built in 1768, resembles a giant pepperpot.
✚ F3 ✉ Haarlemmerweg, near Nieuwpoortkade 🚌 Bus 18

DE GOOIER (FUNENMOLEN)
Amsterdam's most central mill (1725) was the first grain mill in Holland to use the streamlined sails that became ubiquitous. Built on a brick base, with an octagonal body and a thatched wooden frame, it has been converted into a small brewery and bar (▶ 81), but its massive sails still occasionally creak into action.
✚ K5 ✉ Funenkade 🚋 Tram 6, 10; Bus 22, 28

DE RIEKER
The finest windmill in Amsterdam was built in 1636 to drain the Rieker polder, and is situated at the southern tip of the Amstelpark. This was one of Rembrandt's favourite painting locations – there is a small statue nearby in his memory. The windmill has been beautifully preserved and is now a private home.
✚ Off map to south ✉ Amsteldijk, near De Borcht 🚌 Bus 148

National Windmill Day

Windmills have been a feature of the Dutch landscape since the 13th century. Much of the Netherlands lies below sea level, and windmills were used to drain the land and extend the shoreline, creating the fertile farmland called *polder*. Some 950 survive, and on National Windmill Day (the second Saturday in May), many turn their sails and are open to the public.

1100 ROE
This old smock mill, shaped like a peasant's smock, was one of a '*gang*' of water mills that once drained the polders. It stands 1,100 roes from the city's outer canal – the word *roe* means both the flat part of a sail that had to be set or reefed according to wind strength, and a unit of measurement (about 28cm) used to calculate the distance from the city centre.
✚ A5 ✉ Herman Bonpad, Sportpark Ookmeer 🚌 Bus 19, 23

1200 ROE
This early 17th-century post mill, with its impressive platform and revolving cap, was built to help drain the polders.
✚ B3 ✉ Haarlemmerweg, near Willem Molengraaffstraat
🚌 Bus 85

AMSTERDAM
where to...

DUTCH RESTAURANTS

Dutch treats

Numerous restaurants in the city provide a taste of authentic Dutch cuisine. The most delicious dishes include thick split-pea soup (*erwtensoep*), meaty stews (*stamppot*), smoked eel (*gerookt paling*), raw herring (*haring*), sweet and savoury pancakes (*pannekoeken*), waffles (*stroopwafels*) and cheeses. Look out for the special 'Neerlands Dis' sign (a red, white and blue soup tureen), which indicates restaurants commended by this organisation for their top-quality traditional Dutch cuisine.

A recent trend is towards 'New Dutch' cuisine. Traditional dishes are prepared with a lighter touch and presented with greater sophistication, using fresh seasonal products and an adventurous mix of herbs and spices.

DE BLAUWE HOLLANDER (£)

Generous portions of wholesome and modestly priced, if not exactly inspired, fare in a lively bistro setting.

⊞ G6 ⊠ Leidsekruisstraat 28
☎ 6233014 🕐 Dinner only
🚋 Tram 1, 2, 5, 6, 7, 10, 20

DORRIUS (£££)

A sophisticated take on rustic Dutch style. Try the pike and salted cod traditional delicacies, or the cheese soufflé.

⊞ H4 ⊠ Crowne Plaza Hotel, Nieuwezijds Voorburgwal 5
☎ 4202224 🚋 Tram 1, 2, 5, 13, 17, 20

DE GEUS (£)

Dutch pea soup, herring in *jenever* (gin) and warm cheesecake in a wood-panelled 1885 interior.

⊞ G6 ⊠ Korte Leidsedwarsstraat 71
☎ 6271808 🚋 Tram 1, 2, 5, 6, 7, 10, 20

HAESJE CLAES (££)

Dutch cuisine at its best, served in a warren of small, panelled dining rooms. The building dates from the 16th century, and the rooms are authentically furnished.

⊞ G5 ⊠ Spoistraat 73–275
☎ 6249998 🚋 Tram 1, 2, 5

DE KEUKEN VAN 1870 (£)

Originally a soup kitchen, this old-fashioned establishment serves huge platefuls of no-frills food at communal tables.

⊞ H4 ⊠ Spuistraat 4
☎ 6248965 🕐 Mon–Fri 12:30–8; Sat, Sun 4–9 🚋 Tram 1, 2, 5, 13, 17, 20

MOLEN DE DIKKERT (£££)

Dine in a majestic old windmill on the outskirts of Amsterdam.

⊞ Off map to south
⊠ Amsterdamseweg 104
☎ 6411378 🕐 Closed Sun and lunch Sat 🚌 Bus 175

DE POORT (££)

Since 1870, this famous restaurant has sold nearly 6 million numbered steaks. Every thousandth one comes with a free bottle of house wine.

⊞ H5 ⊠ Hotel Die Port van Cleve, Nieuwezijds Voorburgwal 178 ⊠ 6240047 🚋 Tram 1, 2, 5, 13, 17, 20

DE ROODE LEEUW (££)

The brasserie-style 'Red Lion' serves up stews and sauerkraut dishes that are particularly good value.

⊞ H5 ⊠ Amsterdam Hotel, Damrak 93–94 ☎ 5550666
🕐 10AM–midnight, last orders 8PM 🚋 Tram 4, 9, 16, 20, 24, 25

'T SWARTE SCHAEP (££)

The 'Black Sheep' is noted for its rustic atmosphere, excellent wines and varied classic and modern cuisine.

⊞ G6 ⊠ Korte Leidsedwarsstraat 24
☎ 6223021 🚋 Tram 1, 2, 5, 6, 7, 10, 20

D'VIJFF VLIEGHEN (£££)

The menu in the 'Five Flies' in five 17th-century houses has an impressive collection of 'New Dutch' dishes.

⊞ G5 ⊠ Spuistraat 294–302
☎ 6248369 🕐 Dinner only
🚋 Tram 1, 2, 5

ELEGANT DINING

BEDDINGTON'S (£££)

Chef Jean Beddington's imaginative French and Far Eastern cuisine in a strikingly modern setting.
🕂 G7 ✉ Roelof Hartstraat 6–8 ☎ 6765201 🕔 Closed Sun and lunch Sat and Mon 🚊 Tram 3, 5, 12, 20, 24

DE BELHAMEL (££)

Art nouveau and classical music set the tone for polished Continental cuisine in an intimate, often crowded setting with a superb canal view.
🕂 G4 ✉ Brouwersgracht 60 ☎ 6221095 🕔 Dinner only 🚊 Bus 18, 22

BORDEWIJK (££)

Mediterranean and Asian touches, and a spare, black-and-white interior, add zest to French dishes.
🕂 G4 ✉ Noordermarkt 7 ☎ 6243899 🕔 Dinner only. Closed Mon 🚊 Bus 18, 22

CAFÉ ROUX (££)

Fine French cuisine in an art nouveau setting, overlooked by a Karl Appel mural.
🕂 H5 ✉ Grand Hotel, Oudezijds Voorburgwal 197 ☎ 5553560 🚇 Nieuwmarkt

CHRISTOPHE'S (£££)

Chef Jean Christophe combines French style and US experience to great effect in his chic canalside restaurant.
🕂 G4 ✉ Leliegracht 46 ☎ 6250807 🕔 Dinner only. Closed Sun and Mon 🚊 Tram 13, 14, 17, 20

LE CIEL BLEU (£££)

The height of stylish French cuisine on the Okura Hotel's 23rd floor.
🕂 H7 ✉ Ferdinand Bolstraat 333 ☎ 6787111 🕔 Dinner only 🚊 Tram 12, 25

DE GOUDEN REAEL (££)

French restaurant in a 17th-century dockside building with a waterside terrace – perfect for a romantic evening.
🕂 H3 ✉ Zandhoek 14, Westerdok ☎ 6233883 🕔 Closed Sun 🚊 Bus 28, Tram 3

LA RIVE (£££)

In Amsterdam's most expensive hotel. Robert Kranenborg is considered Holland's finest chef.
🕂 J6 ✉ Amstel Hotel, Professor Tulpplein 1 ☎ 6226060 🚇 Weesperplein

DE SILVEREN SPIEGEL (£££)

An exquisite classic menu, complemented by one of the city's best wine lists, in a superbly restored 1614 house. Fish is a speciality.
🕂 H4 ✉ Kattengat 4–6 ☎ 6246589 🕔 Dinner only. Closed Sun except for parties with reservations 🚊 Tram 1, 2, 5, 13, 17, 20

TOUT COURT (£££)

This arty restaurant is a place to see and be seen.
🕂 G5 ✉ Runstraat 13 ☎ 6258637 🕔 Dinner only 🚊 Tram 1, 2, 5

HET TUYNHUIS (££)

Sophisticated French, Portuguese and Dutch cuisine in a converted coach house and garden.
🕂 H5 ✉ Reguliersdwarsstraat 28 ☎ 6276603 🕔 Closed Sat and Sun lunch 🚊 Tram 4, 9, 14, 16, 20, 24, 25

Opening times and prices

The restaurants listed on pages 62–68 are all open for lunch and dinner daily unless otherwise stated. They are divided into three price categories. For a main dish, expect to pay:

£££ over f50
££ up to f50
£ up to f25

Tipping

Most restaurant windows display menus giving the price of individual dishes including BTW (tax) and a 15 per cent service charge. Nevertheless, most Amsterdammers round up a small bill to the largest whole guilder and larger ones to the nearest f5. This tip should be left as change rather than included on a credit-card payment.

INDONESIAN RESTAURANTS

A hearty meal

When the Dutch took over the Spice Islands of the East Indies in the 17th century, they got more than spices out of their new colony. They developed a taste for the exotic local cuisine that survived Indonesian independence and gives Amsterdam today an abundance of *Indonesisch* restaurants.

First-timers to an Indonesian restaurant should order a *rijsttafel*, which includes rice and a complete range of other dishes: *ayam* (chicken), *ikam* (fish), *telor* (egg), *rendang* (beef), *krupuk* (shrimp crackers), shredded coconut and sweet-and-sour vegetables. The *rijsttafel* ('rice table') originally referred to the long list of ingredients required to prepare such a feast. It originated in early colonial days among hungry Dutch planters who, not satisfied by the basic Indonesian meal of rice and vegetables accompanied by meat or fish, continually added other dishes. Thus the rijsttafel was born — a meal that ranges from a 6- to 10-item mini-rijsttafel to a 20- to 30-dish feast.

ANEKA RASA (££)

This airy modern restaurant offers numerous vegetarian dishes including an all-vegetarian *rijsttafel*.

✚ H5 ⊠ Warmoesstraat 25–29 ☎ 6261560
Ⓔ Centraal Station

INDRAPURA (££)

A popular colonial-style restaurant. Tell the waiter how hot and spicy you want your dishes to be.

✚ H5 ⊠ Rembrandtplein 40-42 ☎ 6237329 Ⓓ Dinner only Ⓔ Tram 4, 9, 14, 20

JAYAKARTA (££)

In the square that is one of Amsterdam's liveliest nightlife districts; ideal for late-evening meals.

✚ H5 ⊠ Rembrandtplein 16 ☎ 6255569 Ⓔ Tram 4, 9, 14, 20

KANTJIL EN DE TIJGER (££)

Modern decor and spicy, imaginative Javanese cuisine. Try the delicious *Masi Rames*, a mini-*rijsttafel* on one plate.

✚ G5 ⊠ Spuistraat 291 ☎ 6200994 Ⓓ Dinner only Ⓔ Tram 1, 2, 5

ORIENT (££)

This dark, opulent restaurant specialises in *rijsttafels*, with more than 20 different sorts, three of them vegetarian, and an extensive buffet on Wednesdays.

✚ G6 ⊠ Van Baerlestraat 21 ☎ 6734958 Ⓓ Dinner only Ⓔ Tram 2, 3, 5, 12, 20

SAHID JAYA (££)

Shady courtyard garden, especially nice in summer.

✚ H5 ⊠ Reguliersdwarsstraat 26 ☎ 6263727 Ⓔ Tram 16, 24, 25

SAMA SEBO (££)

Rush mats and batik typify this Balinese setting where you can select from the menu to create your own *rijsttafel*.

✚ G6 ⊠ P C Hooftstraat 27 ☎ 6628146 Ⓓ Closed Sun Ⓔ Tram 2, 5, 20

SARANG MAS (££)

Modern surroundings counterpoint traditional cuisine.

✚ H4 ⊠ Damrak 44 ☎ 6222105 Ⓓ Daily 11.30–11pm Ⓔ Tram 1, 2, 4, 5, 9, 13, 16, 17, 20, 24, 25

SPECIAAL (££)

One of the most popular Indonesian restaurants in town, a cosy little place hidden in a back street in the Jordaan. The *rijsttafel* is a sight to behold.

✚ G4 ⊠ Nieuwe Leliestraat 140-142 ☎ 6249706 Ⓓ Dinner only Ⓔ Tram 10, 13, 14, 17, 20

SUKASARI (£)

Colourful batik tablecloths, closely packed tables, generous portions.

✚ H5 ⊠ Damstraat 26-29 ☎ 6240092 Ⓓ Mon–Sat noon–9pm Ⓔ Tram 4, 9, 16, 20, 24, 25

TEMPO DOELOE (££)

One of Amsterdam's best Indonesian restaurants, notable for its western interior, exotic flowers and some of the hottest dishes in town

✚ H6 ⊠ Utrechtsestraat 75 ☎ 6256718 Ⓓ Dinner only Ⓔ Tram 4

FISH & VEGETARIAN RESTAURANTS

BODEGA KEYSER (££)

An Amsterdam institution next door to the Concertgebouw, specialising in fish and traditional Dutch dishes.

⊞ G6 ⊠ Van Baerlestraat 96 ☎ 6711441 ⓒ Mon–Sat 9AM–midnight; Sun 11AM–midnight ⊟ Tram 2, 3, 5, 12, 20

DE OESTERBAR (££)

The seasonal delights of this elegant fish restaurant include herring in May, mussels in June and delicate Zeeland oysters throughout the summer.

⊞ G6 ⊠ Leidseplein 10 ☎ 6232988 ⊟ Tram 1, 2, 5, 6, 7, 10, 20

LE PECHEUR (£££)

A chic fish-bistro with a secluded garden. Outstanding fresh oysters, caviar, sashimi and lobster.

⊞ H5 ⊠ Reguliersdwarsstraat 32 ☎ 6243121 ⓒ Closed Sat lunch and all day Sun ⊟ Tram 1, 2, 5

PIER 10 (££)

Former shipping office with an innovative menu that emphasises fish, and an unusual shipside location on Pier 10 behind Centraal Station – one of the series of jetties where ships dock on the IJ inlet.

⊞ H4 ⊠ De Ruijterkade, Pier 10 ☎ 6248276 ⓒ Dinner only ⊟ Tram 1, 2, 4, 5, 9, 13, 16, 17, 20, 24, 25 ⓠ Centraal Station

VISRESTAURANT JULIA (££)

Julia's famous fish platter, with 10 kinds of fish – baked, barbecued and grilled – draws people from all over the region.

⊞ Off map to south ⊠ Amstelveenseweg 160 ☎ 6795394 ⓒ Dinner only ⊟ Bus 146, 147, 170, 171, 172

VEGETARIAN

BENTO (££)

Japanese fish and organic vegetable dishes, tatami mats.

⊞ H6 ⊠ Kerkstraat 148 ☎ 4203485 ⓒ Closed Mon ⊟ Tram 16, 24, 25

BOLHOED (£)

A trendy restaurant on the edge of the Jordaan, with vegetarian pâtés, salads and hearty dishes.

⊞ G4 ⊠ Prinsengracht 60-62 ☎ 6261803 ⊟ Tram 13, 14, 17, 20

GOLDEN TEMPLE (£)

Imaginative menu of Indian, Mexican and Middle Eastern dishes.

⊞ H6 ⊠ Utrechtsestraat 126 ☎ 6268560 ⓒ Dinner only ⊟ Tram 4

HEMELSE MODDER (££)

Sophisticated main courses including a vegetarian selection and delicious desserts including 'Heavenly Mud', the chocolate mousse from which the restaurant takes its name.

⊞ H5 ⊠ Oude Waal 211 ☎ 6243203 ⓒ Dinner only 6–10 (last admission). Closed Tue ⓠ Nieuwmarkt

OIBIBIO (££)

New Age music sets the tone for laid-back world cuisine in chic setting.

⊞ H4 ⊠ Prins Hendrikkade 20-21 ☎ 5539328 ⓠ Centraal Station

Fish and vegetables

Although the Dutch eat a lot of meat, Amsterdam with its sea-going associations has a great choice of fish restaurants. Vegetarians, too, have specialist eating places to suit all tastes and budgets, while others, most notably pizzerias and the Asian restaurants around town, offer vegetarian menu-dishes.

INTERNATIONAL RESTAURANTS

Surinamese cuisine

Explore the narrow streets of the multi-racial district around Albert Cuypstraat, and you will soon realise how easy it is to eat your way around the world in Amsterdam. The many Surinamese restaurants here serve a delicious blend of African, Chinese and Indian cuisine. Specialties include *bojo* (cassava and coconut quiche) and *pitjil* (baked vegetables with peanut sauce). Try them at Marowijne (⊠ Albert Cuypstraat 68–70), or Wan Pipel (⊠ Albert Cuypstraat 140).

ASIAN CARIBBEAN EXPERIENCE (£)

More than 100 dishes from all over Asia and the Caribbean.

✚ H5 ⊠ Warmoesstraat 170 ☎ 6271545 🕐 Dinner only 🚃 Tram 4, 9, 16, 20, 24, 25

DE BRAKKE GROND (£–££)

Flemish Cultural Centre's darkly atmospheric restaurant, serving bountiful portions of Belgian food.

✚ H5 ⊠ Nes 43 ☎ 6260044 🕐 Tue–Sat noon–11. Closed Sun–Mon 🚃 Tram 4, 9, 14, 16, 20, 24, 25

BRASSERIE RENTRÉE (££)

An eclectic menu of French, Asian and Dutch dishes, in a romantic, candlelit setting.

✚ H4 ⊠ Zeedijk 29 ☎ 6389340 🕐 Daily, dinner only 5:30–11 (last admission) 🚇 Centraal Station

CAFÉ PACIFICO (££)

The most authentic Mexican bodega in town. Especially crowded on Tuesday, which is *margarita* night.

✚ H4 ⊠ Warmoesstraat 31 ☎ 6242911 🕐 Dinner only 🚇 Centraal Station

CHEZ GEORGES (££)

Fine Belgian cuisine in a classical, candlelit setting.

✚ G4 ⊠ Herenstraat 3 ☎ 6263332 🕐 Closed Sun, Wed 🚃 Tram 1, 2, 5, 13, 17, 20

DYNASTY (£££)

A sophisticated, sumptuously decorated garden restaurant with fine Southeast Asian cuisine.

✚ H5 ⊠ Reguliersdwarsstraat 30 ☎ 6268400 🕐 Dinner only. Closed Tue 🚃 Tram 16, 24, 25

EL RANCHO ARGENTINIAN GRILL (££)

Sizzling steaks and spare ribs in a wood-panelled, jolly-gaucho setting that brings a taste of the pampas to Amsterdam.

✚ H5 ⊠ Spui 3 ☎ 6256764 🕐 11AM–midnight 🚃 Tram 4, 9, 14, 16, 20, 24, 25

DE FLES BISTRO (££)

Cosy cellar, full of large wooden tables. A real locals' hangout.

✚ H6 ⊠ Vijzelstraat 137 ☎ 6249644 🕐 Dinner only 🚃 Tram 16, 24, 25

FROMAGERIE CRIGNON CULINAIR (£)

Rustic restaurant with eight different types of cheese fondue.

✚ H5 ⊠ Gravenstraat 28 ☎ 6246428 🕐 6AM–9.30PM. Closed Sun, Mon 🚃 Tram 4, 9, 16, 20, 24, 25

GAUGUIN (££)

Exotic mix of Eastern and Western dishes; colourful South Seas setting.

✚ G6 ⊠ Leidsekade 110 ☎ 6221526 🕐 Dinner only. Closed Mon, Tue 🚃 Tram 1, 2, 5, 6, 7, 10, 20

MEMORIES OF INDIA (££)

Tandoori, Moghlai and vegetarian cuisine in refined colonial setting.

✚ H5 ⊠ Reguliersdwarsstraat 88 ☎ 6235710 🕐 Dinner only 🚃 Tram 4, 9, 14, 20

PAKISTAN (££)
Holland's top Pakistani restaurant. The menu ranges from traditional, village dishes to highly spiced specialities.

✚ F5 ✉ De Clercqstraat 65 ☎ 6181120 🕐 Dinner only 🚋 Tram 3, 12, 13, 14

PASTA E BASTA (££)
Pasta in chic surroundings, with opera classics.

✚ G6 ✉ Nieuwe Spiegelstraat 8 ☎ 4222229 🚋 Tram 16, 24, 25

ROSE'S CANTINA (££)
Excellent value Tex-Mex meals in lively, sociable surroundings. Probably Amsterdam's most crowded restaurant.

✚ H5 ✉ Reguliersdwarsstraat 38–40 ☎ 6259797 🕐 Dinner only 🚋 Tram 16, 24, 25

RUM RUNNERS (££)
Giant palms, caged parrots, live music, spicy stews and cocktails feel distinctly tropical.

✚ G4 ✉ Prinsengracht 277 ☎ 6274079 🕐 Mon–Fri from 4PM. Sat, Sun from 2PM 🚋 Tram 13, 14, 17, 20

SAUDADE (££)
A Portuguese restaurant with dockside terrace, at the heart of the fashionable Entrepotdok district.

✚ L5 ✉ Entrepotdok 36 ☎ 6254845 🕐 Dinner only. Closed Tue 🚌 Bus 22

SHERPA (£)
Nepalese/Tibetan restaurant with traditional Himalayan ornaments.

✚ G6 ✉ Korte Leidsedwarsstraat 58 ☎ 6239495 🕐 Dinner only 🚋 Tram 1, 2, 5, 6, 7, 10, 20

SHIBLI (£££)
Sit on a sofa inside a Bedouin tent, dining on an Arabian banquet.

✚ H5 ✉ Hotel Krasnapolsky, Dam 9 ☎ 4223291 🕐 Thu–Sun dinner. Closed Mon–Thu, lunch 🚋 Tram 4, 9, 14, 16, 20, 24, 25

SUKHOTHAI (££)
Thai dishes in bamboo and palm surroundings. Try the special Nua Pad Prik Bai Kra Pauw – if you can pronounce it!

✚ H7 ✉ Ceintuurbaan 147 ☎ 6718086 🕐 Dinner only Closed Tue 🚋 Tram 3

TANGO (££)
Small, candlelit, and on the edge of the Red Light District. Try the huge, juicy steaks.

✚ H4 ✉ Warmoesstraat 49 ☎ 6272467 🕐 Dinner only 🚋 Tram 4, 9, 16, 20, 24, 25

TEPPANYAKI NIPPON (££)
One of Holland's most elegant and exclusive Japanese grill-restaurants.

✚ H5 ✉ Reguliersdwarsstraat 18–20 ☎ 6208787 🕐 Dinner only 🚋 Tram 16, 24, 25

TOSCANINI (££)
The best Italian food in town. Book well ahead.

✚ G4 ✉ Lindengracht 75 ☎ 6232813 🕐 Dinner only 🚋 Tram 3

LE ZINC...ET LES DAMES (££)
Home-style French cuisine in a converted canalside warehouse. The *tarte tatin* is superb.

✚ H6 ✉ Prinsengracht 999 ☎ 6229044 🕐 Dinner only. Closed Sun, Mon 🚋 Tram 4

A taste of China
Of the many superb Chinese restaurants in the city, one of the most popular is Treasure (✉ Nieuwezijds Voorburgwal 115–17), with specialities from Beijing, Shanghai and Canton provinces. For something inexpensive but good, try Sichuan (✉ Lange Niezel 24), with its unusual Tibetan and Szechuan dishes. The Sea Palace (✉ Oosterdokskade 8), advertises itself as Europe's first floating restaurant. It is modelled on a Chinese pagoda-style palace and is the next best thing to its prototype, Hong Kong's famous *Jumbo* restaurant.

SNACKS & *EETCAFÉS*

A bite to 'eet'

Try an *eetcafé* for filling homemade fare – soup, sandwiches and omelettes. Remember that kitchens close around 9PM. Or browse market stalls for local delicacies. Most bars offer *borrelhapjes* (mouthfuls with a glass) – usually olives, chunks of cheese or *borrelnoten* (nuts with a savoury coating). More substantial *borrelhapjes* are *bitterballen* (bitter balls) – fried balls of vegetable paste; and *vlamaetjes* (little flames) – spicy mini spring rolls. For a really quick snack, the many Febo company's food dispensers about town are cheap: simply put your money in and your snack comes out hot.

CAFÉ DANTZIG (£)
Giant, crusty baguettes with delicious fillings make a perfect lunch on the terrace beside the Amstel river.

H5 ✉ Zwanenburgwal 15
☎ 6209039 🕔 10AM–1AM
🚊 Waterlooplein

CAFÉ KORT (££)
A delightfully located café-cum-restaurant on the corner of Prinsengracht and Reguliersgracht, with a charming shady terrace beside the canals.

H6 ✉ Amstelveld 12
☎ 6261199 🕔 Closed Tue
🚊 Tram 4

GARY'S MUFFINS (£)
A late-night snack shop in a street of trendy bars and clubs. Also open during the day.

H5 ✉ Reguliersdwarsstraat 53 ☎ 4202406 🕔 11AM–3AM (Fri, Sat 4AM) 🚊 Tram 4, 9, 14, 16, 20, 24, 25

KAAS-WIJNHUIS (£)
A charming delicatessen-cum-*eetcafé* with wines, cheeses, cold cuts, pâtés.

H4 ✉ Warmoesstraat 16
☎ 6230878 🕔 Mon–Sat 9–6; Sun noon–6 🚊 Centraal Station

LUNCHROOM DIALOGUE (£)
A warehouse cellar, away from the crowds at Anne Frankhuis next door; good for sandwiches and cakes.

G4 ✉ Prinsengracht 261a
☎ 6239991 🕔 Daily 10–5
🚊 Tram 13, 14, 17

MORITA-YA (£)
Traditional Japanese snackbar with floor seating as well as tables, that's a must for sushi fans.

H4 ✉ Zeedijk 18
☎ 6380756 🕔 Dinner only. Closed Wed 🚊 Centraal Station

PANCAKE BAKERY (£)
The best pancakes in town, cooked on an old Dutch griddle.

G5 ✉ Prinsengracht 191
☎ 6251333 🚊 Tram 13, 14, 17, 20

LA PLACE (£)
A self-service 'indoor market' restaurant. Choose your dish at one of the stands, watch it being cooked, then eat at one of the tables.

H5 ✉ Rokin 164
☎ 6202364 🕔 9AM–9PM except Thu 9AM–10PM, Sun noon–9PM 🚊 Tram 4, 9, 14, 16, 20, 24, 25

SMALL TALK (££)
Near the Museumplein, this *eetcafé* is ideal for soups and snacks between gallery visits.

G6 ✉ Van Baerlestraat 52
☎ 6714864 🚊 Tram 2, 3, 5, 12, 20

TAPAS CATALÀ (£)
Enjoy a quick bite or a meal of tempting Catalan tapas dishes.

G5 ✉ Spuistraat 299
☎ 6231141 🕔 Dinner only. Closed Tue 🚊 Tram 1, 2, 5

VAN DOBBEN (£)
A renowned sandwich shop. Try the meat croquette roll that Van Dobben himself makes from a 53-year-old recipe.

H5 ✉ Korte Reguliersdwarsstraat 5–9
☎ 6244200 🕔 Mon–Thu 9:30AM–1PM; Fri–Sat 9:30AM–2PM; Sun 11:30AM–8PM
🚊 Tram 4, 9, 14

CAFÉS & TEA SHOPS

BACKSTAGE (£)

A wacky, psychedelic café run by an eccentric entertainer.

✚ H6 ✉ Utrechtsedwarsstraat 67 ☎ 6223638 🕐 10–5:30. Closed Sun 🚃 Tram 4

CAFÉ AMÉRICAIN (£)

Artists, writers and bohemians frequent this grand art deco café.

✚ G6 ✉ American Hotel, Leidseplein 28 ☎ 6245322 🕐 7AM–1AM 🚃 Tram 1, 2, 5, 6, 7, 10, 20

CAFÉ ESPRIT

Designer café, all glass and aluminum, run by the clothing chain next door; popular stop for shoppers.

✚ H5 ✉ Spui 10a ☎ 6221967 🕐 Mon–Sat 10–6 (Thu until 10PM); Sun noon–6 🚃 Tram 1, 2, 4, 5, 9, 14, 16, 20, 24, 25

CAFÉ VERTIGO (££)

Brown café-style surroundings, where menu-dishes occasionally reflect themes at the nearby Film Museum.

✚ G6 ✉ Vondelpark 3 ☎ 6123021 🚃 Tram 1, 3, 6, 12

GELATERIA JORDINO (£)

Bright and breezy place that does great home-made Italian ice-cream and waistline-threatening chocolate cake.

✚ H4 ✉ Haarlemmerdijk 25 ☎ 4203225 🚌 Bus 18, 22

GREENWOOD'S (£)

Homely little English-style tearoom serving up scones with jam and cream, chocolate cake and lemon-meringue pie.

✚ H4 ✉ Singel 103 ☎ 6237071 🕐 Daily 9:30–7 🚃 Tram 1, 2, 5, 13, 17, 20

METZ (£)

Views from the top floor café of this department store (▶ 71) are among the city's finest.

✚ G5 ✉ Keizersgracht 455 ☎ 5207048 🚃 Tram 1, 2, 5

NIEUWE KAFÉ (£)

The café's crowded terrace on Dam square provides a captive audience for buskers; ideal for people-watching.

✚ H5 ✉ Eggertstraat 8 ☎ 6272830 🕐 8:30–6 🚃 Tram 4, 9, 14, 16, 20, 24, 25

POMPADOUR (£)

The finest chocolatier in town doubles as a sumptuous tearoom.

✚ G5 ✉ Huidenstraat 12 ☎ 6239554 🕐 Mon 1–6; Tue–Sat 9–6 🚃 Tram 1, 2, 5

LA RUCHE (£)

Treat yourself to coffee with waffles piled high with strawberries and cream in this café in De Bijenkorf department store (▶ 72), overlooking Dam square.

✚ H5 ✉ 1 Dam ☎ 6218080 🕐 Mon–Sat 9:30–6, except Thu 9:30–9, Sun noon–6 🚃 Tram 4, 9, 14, 16, 20, 24, 25

WINKEL (£)

A popular café looking out on to the Noordermarkt (▶ 53). Great for people-watching when the markets are on.

✚ G4 ✉ Noordermarkt 43 ☎ 6230223 🕐 Closed evenings and Sun 🚃 Tram 3, 10

Coffee shops

In Amsterdam, the expression 'coffee shop' refers to the 'smoking' coffee shops, where mostly young people hang out, high on hash. 'Smoking' coffee shops are usually easily recognisable by their psychedelic decor, thick fog of bitter smoke and mellow clientele. The cake on sale is sure to be drug-laced 'space cake'. Surprisingly, many such shops do a good cup of coffee.

SHOPPING AREAS

Shopping tips

Although Amsterdam does not compare with Paris or London for European chic, the large number of unusual specialist stores, secondhand shops and colourful markets among its more than 10,000 shops and department stores, make shopping a real pleasure. Interesting souvenirs and gifts to take home are easy to find, whatever your budget. Most shops are open Tuesday to Saturday from 9AM or 10AM until 6PM, on Mondays from 1PM until 6PM, on Thursdays until 9PM. Many shops open noon–5PM on Sundays too. Cash is the usual method of payment, although credit cards and Eurocheques are accepted at most department stores and larger shops.

Dutch gifts

Bulbs

Made-to-measure clogs

Bottle of *jenever* (Dutch gin)

Edam or Gouda cheese

Diamonds

Leerdam crystal

Makkum pottery

An old print or map of the city

Delftware – if you want the real thing look for De Porcelyne Fles (see panel ► 21)

ART & ANTIQUES

Antique shops are concentrated in the *Spiegelkwartier* near the Museumplein, along and by Nieuwe Spiegelstraat, and along the Rokin. Countless galleries are scattered throughout the city, although many can be found along the main canals. The De Looier Kunst- & Antiekcentrum on Elandsgracht in the Jordaan brings together dozens of art and antiques dealers in an indoor market. Other places to buy art, though not originals, are museum shops that sell high-quality poster reproductions of the famous artworks on their walls, by both Dutch and international artists. Look for the best of these at the Rijksmuseum, Van Gogh Museum, Stedelijk Museum of Modern Art and Museum het Rembrandthuis.

BOOKSHOPS

Most bookshops, including the American Book Centre and a branch of British chain Waterstone's in Kalverstraat, are around the university district (off the Spui) and in Leidsestraat. You will also find several specialist antique bookshops on Nieuwezijds Voorburgwal, and there is an indoor antiquarian book market at Oudemanhuispoort.

FASHION

The three main shopping thoroughfares – Kalverstraat, Nieuwendijk and Leidsestraat – are lined with international chain stores and mainstream outlets for clothing and accessories. To the south, you'll find designer stores, including Armani, Azorro and Rodier, along P C Hooftstraat, van Baerlestraat and Beethovenstraat. For more adventurous garb, head for the Jordaan.

OFFBEAT SHOPS

Tiny specialist shops and boutiques selling everything from psychedelic mushrooms to designer soap and kitsch toilet furniture can be found all over the city. Many are in the Jordaan and along the web of side streets that connect the ring canals between Leidsegracht and Brouwersgracht.

SECONDHAND

Explore the secondhand shops of the Jordaan for a bargain, or sift through local street markets, including the city's largest and wackiest fleamarket at Waterlooplein.

SHOPPING MALLS

There are five main shopping malls: chic Magna Plaza near Dam square; De Amsterdamse Poort, reached by metro at Amsterdam Zuidoost; Winkelcentrum Boven't IJ, reached by ferry across the IJ; Winkelcentrum Amstelveen in the southern suburbs, reached by tram 5; and Schiphol Plaza at the airport, open from 7AM until 10PM daily.

DUTCH SOUVENIRS

**AMSTERDAM
SMALLEST GALLERY**
An original painting of the
city bought here will
remind you of your stay.
✚ G4 ✉ Westermarkt 60
☎ 6223756 🚊 Tram 13, 14,
17, 20

BLUE GOLD FISH
Storehouse of fantastical
gifts including jewellery,
ornaments, home fixtures
and fabrics.
✚ G5 ✉ Rozengracht 17
☎ 6233134 🚊 Tram 13, 14,
17, 20

BONEBAKKER
Holland's royal jewellers,
with dazzling displays of
gold and silverware.
Enjoyable even if you
can't afford to buy.
✚ H5 ✉ Rokin 88–90
☎ 6232294 🚊 Tram 4, 9, 14,
16, 20, 24, 25

**DAM SQUARE
SOUVENIRS**
Centrally-located souvenir
shop with a wide choice of
clogs, furnishings, pottery
and T-shirts.
✚ H5 ✉ Dam 17
☎ 6203432 🚊 Tram 4, 9, 14,
16, 20, 24, 25

FOCKE & MELTZER
A superior gift shop, with
Delft Blue porcelain from
De Porceleyne Fles, as well
as outstanding Tichelaars
Makkumware pottery,
Leerdam crystal and
locally made silver.
✚ G6 ✉ P C Hooftstraat 65-
67 ☎ 6642311 🚊 Tram 2, 3,
5, 12, 20

**HEINEN
HANDPAINTED
DELFTWARE**
Tiny but delightful for its
Delftware plates, tulip
vases and Christmas
decorations.
✚ G4 ✉ Prinsengracht 440
☎ 6278299 🚊 Tram 1, 2, 5,
13, 17, 20

**HOLLAND GALLERY
DE MUNT**
Miniature ceramic canal
houses, dolls in traditional
costume, ornately
decorated wooden boxes,
and trays.
✚ H5 ✉ Muntplein 12
☎ 6232271 🚊 Tram 4, 9, 14,
16, 24, 25

HET KANTENHUIS
Exquisite handmade
Dutch lace.
✚ H5 ✉ Kalverstraat 124
☎ 6248618 🚊 Tram 4, 9, 14,
16, 20, 24, 25

DE KLOMPENBOER
Authentic clog factory
offers the city's largest
selection of hand-crafted
footwear.
✚ H4 ✉ Nieuwzijds
Voorburgwal 20 ☎ 6230632
🚊 Tram 1, 2, 5, 13, 17, 20

METZ & CO
Expensive gifts and
designer furniture. One
of the city's most stylish
department stores. It has
a café on the top floor
(► 69).
✚ G5 ✉ Keizersgracht 455
☎ 6248810 🚊 Tram 1, 2, 5

DE TUIN
The Bloemenmarkt
(► 38) is the cheapest
place to buy bulbs and
this stall has the widest
selection.
✚ H5 ✉ Bloemenmarkt
(opposite Singel 502)
☎ 6254571 🚊 Tram 4, 9, 14,
16, 20, 24, 25

Tax-free shopping

If you live outside the European
Union, you may claim a tax
refund of 13.5 per cent on
purchases of f300 or more in one
shop in one day. At shops bearing
the 'Tax Free Shopping' logo, ask
for a Global Refund Cheque when
you pay.

You must export your purchases
within 3 months of buying them.
At departure to a non-European
Union country, go to Customs and
present your purchases and
receipts to have your Global
Refund Cheque validated. You can
obtain a cash refund in Schiphol's
departure hall, or arrange for a
charge-card credit or certified
cheque. You should allow around
an hour to do this.

If you are travelling by train or
car from Holland, you need to go
through this procedure at your
point of exit from the European
Union (if you want to take
advantage of the refund scheme).
You cannot validate the shopping
cheque at Holland's borders with
neighbouring countries, because
they are EU members.

FOOD, DRINK & DEPARTMENT STORES

Say cheese!

Think Dutch cheese and the distinctive red *Edammer* (from Edam) and *Goudse* (from Gouda) spring to mind. They can be young (*jong*) and mild, or more mature (*belegen*) and strong. Mild young cheeses such as *Leerdammer* and *Maaslander* deserve a tasting, too. Others to try are *Friese Nagelkaas*, flavoured with cumin and cloves and *Gras Kaas* (grass cheese), sold in summer, which owes its especially creamy flavour to the freshness of spring's cow pastures.

DE BIERKONING
850 beers and glasses from around the world.
H5 ✉ Paleisstraat 125
☎ 6252336 🚊 Tram 1, 2, 5, 13, 14, 17, 20

DE BIJENKORF
Amsterdam's busy main department store, the *Bijenkorf* ('Beehive') lives up to its name.
H5 ✉ Dam 1
☎ 6218080 🚊 Tram 4, 9, 14, 16, 20, 24, 25

EICHHOLTZ
Established delicatessen with Dutch, American and English specialities.
G6 ✉ Leidsestraat 48
☎ 6220305 🚊 Tram 1, 2, 5

GEELS EN CO
Holland's oldest coffee roasting and tea trading company, full of heady aromas, with a helpful staff and traditional setting.
H4 ✉ Warmoesstraat 67
☎ 6240683 🚊 Tram 4, 9, 14, 16, 20, 24, 25

HENDRIKSE PATISSERIE
Queen Beatrix buys her pastries here.
F6 ✉ Overtoom 472
☎ 6180472 🚊 Tram 1, 6

H P DE VRENG & ZN
Celebrated wine-and-spirits establishment, producing fine liqueurs and *jenevers* since 1852.
H4 ✉ Nieuwendijk 75
☎ 6244581 🚊 Tram 1, 2, 5, 13, 17, 20

J G BEUNE
Famous for chocolate versions of *Amsterdammertjes* (the

bollards lining the streets to prevent cars parking on the pavement), and a mouth-watering array of cakes and other bonbons.
G4 ✉ Haarlemmerdijk 156–8 ☎ 6248356
🚊 Tram 1, 2, 5, 13, 17, 20

MAISON DE BONNETERIE
A gracious department store, popular with wealthy ladies.
H5 ✉ Rokin 140–2/Kalverstraat 183
☎ 6262162 🚊 Tram 4, 9, 14, 16, 20, 24, 25

VITALS VITAMIN-ADVICE SHOP
Vitamins, minerals and other food supplements, plus a unique service: a computerised vitamin test that proposes vitamin supplements based on your age and lifestyle.
H4 ✉ Nieuwe Nieuwstraat 47 ☎ 6257298 🚊 Tram 1, 2, 5, 13, 17, 20

VROOM & DREESMAN
Clothing, jewellery, perfumes, electronic and household goods.
H5 ✉ Kalverstraat 201–221 ☎ 6220171 🚊 Tram 4, 9, 14, 16, 20, 24, 25

DE WATERWINKEL
A hundred different mineral waters.
G7 ✉ Roelof Hartstraat 10
☎ 6755932 🚊 Tram 3, 12, 20, 24

WOUT ARXHOEK
One of the best cheese shops, with over 250 different varieties.
H5 ✉ Damstraat 19
☎ 6229118 🚊 Tram 4, 9, 14, 16, 20, 24, 25

ANTIQUES & BOOKS

AMERICAN BOOK CENTRE

Four floors of English-language books, plus US and British magazines and newspapers, and games.

✚ H5 ✉ Kalverstraat 185
☎ 6255537 🚊 Tram 4, 9, 14, 16, 20, 24, 25

AMSTERDAM ANTIQUES GALLERY

Six dealers under one roof, selling silver, pewter, paintings and Dutch tiles, among other items.

✚ G6 ✉ Nieuwe Spiegelstraat 34 ☎ 6253371 🚊 Tram 6, 7, 10

ATHENAEUM BOEKHANDEL

This bookshop, in a striking art nouveau building, stocks international newspapers and specialises in social sciences, literature and the classics.

✚ G5 ✉ Spui 14–16
☎ 6226248 🚊 Tram 1, 2, 5

EDUARD KRAMER

Old Dutch tiles, the earliest dating from 1580.

✚ G6 ✉ Nieuwe Spiegelstraat 64 ☎ 6230832 🚊 Tram 6, 7, 10

EGIDIUS ANTIQUARISCHE BOEKHANDEL

A tiny shop packed with antique books on travel, photography and the arts.

✚ H5 ✉ Nieuwezijds Voorburgwal 334 ☎ 6243929
🚊 Tram 1, 2, 5

DE KINDER-BOEKWINKEL

Children's books, arranged according to age.

✚ G5 ✉ Rozengracht 34

☎ 6224761 🚊 Tram 13, 14, 17, 20

LAMBIEK

The world's oldest comic shop.

✚ G6 ✉ Kerkstraat 78
☎ 6267543 🚊 Tram 1, 2, 5

DE LOOIER KUNST- & ANTIEKCENTRUM

A covered antiques market with hundreds of stalls selling everything from quality items to junk.

✚ G5 ✉ Elandsgracht 109
☎ 6249038 🚊 Tram 7, 10, 17, 20

PREMSELA & HAMBURGER

Fine antique jewellery and silver in a refined setting.

✚ H5 ✉ Rokin 120
☎ 6249688 🚊 Tram 4, 9, 16, 20, 24, 25

SCHELTEMA, HOLKEMA EN VERMEULEN

The city's biggest bookshop, with a floor of computer software and audio and video titles.

✚ G5 ✉ Koningsplein 20
☎ 5231411 🚊 Tram 1, 2, 5

DE SLEGTE

Amsterdam's largest secondhand bookshop is good for bargains.

✚ H5 ✉ Kalverstraat 48–52
☎ 6225933 🚊 Tram 4, 9, 14, 16, 20, 24, 25

'T CACHOT

Secondhand thrillers and crime novels in the jail of what was once Holland's smallest police station.

✚ L9 ✉ Dorpsplein
☎ 6691795 🕐 Tue, Wed, Sat afternoons only
🚊 Bus 59, 60, 175

Going, going, gone!

Amsterdam's main auction houses are Sotheby's (✉ Rokin 102 ☎ 5502200) and Christie's (✉ Cornelis Schuytstraat 57 ☎ 5755255). Their Dutch counterpart, Veilinghuis (Auction House) de Nieuwe Zon, is at Overtoom 197 (☎ 6168586). All hold pre-sale viewings, interesting even if you have no intention of buying.

SPECIALIST SHOPS

Magna Plaza

Amsterdam's most luxurious shopping mall, Magna Plaza, is in an imposing neo-Gothic building in Nieuwezijds Voorburgwal near Dam square. Its four floors are filled with upmarket specialist shops, such as Pinokkio, for educational toys; Bjorn Borg, for sporty underwear; and Speeldozenwereld, for quaint musical boxes. There is a café on the top floor and a Virgin Megastore in the basement.

ANIMATION ART
Drawings, paintings and figurines of famous cartoon characters from Superman to Tintin and the Smurfs.
✚ G5 ✉ Berenstraat 19
☎ 6277600 🚋 Tram 1, 2, 5

ART RAGES
The latest in contemporary pottery, jewellery and glass, by mainly European and North American craftspeople.
✚ G6 ✉ Spiegelgracht 2a
☎ 6273645 🚋 Tram 6, 7, 10

DE BEESTENWINKEL
A cuddly-toy shop for adults. Ideal for collectors and small gifts.
✚ H5 ✉ Staalstraat 11
☎ 6231805 🚋 Tram 4, 9, 14, 16, 20, 24, 25

BELLTREE
A toyshop with benign toys, many made from wood, that children should find educational and fun.
✚ G6 ✉ Spiegelgracht 10–12
☎ 6258830 🚋 Tram 6, 7, 10

CHRISTMAS WORLD
Sample the special atmosphere of Christmas in Holland all year round, amid glittering displays of candles and bells.
✚ H5 ✉ Nieuwezijds Voorburgwal 137–9
☎ 6227047 🚋 Tram 1, 2, 5, 13, 17, 20

CONCERTO
Finest all-round selection of new and used records and CDs to suit all tastes. Especially good for jazz, classical music and hits from the '50s and '60s.
✚ H6 ✉ Utrechtsestraat 52–60 ☎ 6245467 🚋 Tram 4

CONSCIOUS DREAMS
Anything's possible in Amsterdam. This shop specialises in 'magic mushrooms'!
✚ H6 ✉ Kerkstraat 117
☎ 6266907 🚋 Tram 16, 24, 25

DEN HAAN & WAGENMAKERS
A quilt-maker's paradise of traditional fabrics, tools and gadgets.
✚ H4 ✉ Nieuwezijds Voorburgwal 97–9 ☎ 6202525
🚋 Tram 1, 2, 5, 13, 17, 20

DE FIETSENMAKER
One of the top bike shops in Amsterdam.
✚ H5 ✉ Nieuwe Hoogstraat 21–23 ☎ 6246137
🚇 Nieuwmarkt

FIFTIES-SIXTIES
A jumble of period pieces including toasters, records, lamps and other mementoes of this hip era.
✚ G5 ✉ Huidenstraat 13
☎ 6232653 🚋 Tram 1, 2, 5

HAIR POLICE
Hair styles of any shape and colour, plus far-out fashion and accessories, at this trendy boutique.
✚ H6 ✉ Kerkstraat 113
☎ 4205841
🚋 Tram 16, 24, 25

HEAD SHOP
The shop for marijuana paraphernalia and memorabilia ever since it opened in the '60s.
✚ H5 ✉ Kloveniersburgwal 39 ☎ 6249061
🚇 Nieuwmarkt

HEMP WORKS
Designer hemp shop: jeans, jackets, shirts,

shampoo and soap all made of hemp.

➕ H4 ✉ Nieuwendijk 13 ☎ 4211762 🚊 Tram 1, 2, 5, 13, 17, 20

JACOB HOOIJ

Old-fashioned apothecary, selling herbs, spices and homeopathic remedies since 1743.

➕ H5 ✉ Kloveniersburgwal 12 ☎ 6243041 🚊 Nieuwmarkt

KITSCH KITCHENS

Ghanaian metal furniture, Indian bead curtains, Mexican tablecloths, Chinese pots and pans – the whole world in one colourful kitchen!

➕ G5 ✉ 1e Bloemdwarsstraat 21 ☎ 4284969 🚊 Tram 13, 14, 17, 20

OTTEN & ZOON

Some Dutch people still clomp around in wooden *klompen* (clogs). This shop makes fine wearable ones as well as souvenirs.

➕ H7 ✉ Eerste Van der Helstraat 6 ☎ 6629724 🚊 Tram 16, 24, 25

OUTRAS COISAS

Ancient and modern pots and gardening tools, reflecting the Dutch passion for plants.

➕ G4 ✉ Herenstraat 31 ☎ 6257281 🚊 Tram 1, 2, 5, 13, 14, 17, 20

PARTY HOUSE

A cornucopia of paper decorations, dressing-up clothes, masks and practical jokes.

➕ G5 ✉ Rozengracht 93a–b ☎ 6247851 🚊 Tram 13, 14, 17, 20

PAS-DESTOEL

Furniture and interiors designed with a touch of innocent fantasy for children.

➕ G4 ✉ Westerstraat 260 ☎ 4207542 🚊 Tram 3, 10

P G C HAJENIUS

One of the world's finest tobacco shops, in elegant, art deco premises.

➕ H5 ✉ Rokin 92–96 ☎ 6237494 🚊 Tram 4, 9, 14, 16, 20, 24, 25

RED EARTH

Pamper yourself with exotic body-care products made from natural ingredients and essential oils according to ancient Aboriginal recipes.

➕ G6 ✉ Leidsestraat 64 ☎ 6221620 🚊 Tram 1, 2, 5

SCALE TRAIN HOUSE

Take home a windmill or canal barge DIY kit as a souvenir, or choose from the vast stock of model railway components.

➕ F5 ✉ Bilderdijkstraat 94 ☎ 6122670 🚊 Tram 3, 12, 13, 14

DE SPEELMUIS

A splendid collection of handmade wooden toys and doll's house miniatures.

➕ G5 ✉ Elandsgracht 58 ☎ 6385342 🚊 Tram 7, 10, 17, 20

WORLD OF WONDERS

Interior design shop in the fast-gentrifying Eastern Docks area, with high class fabrics and furnishings, and many small items to enliven your living space.

➕ L4 ✉ KNSM-Laan 293 ☎ 4634069 🚊 Bus 32

Oibibio

This department store-cum-spiritual centre (✉ Prins Hendrikkade 20–21) offers environmentally friendly clothing (in cotton, wool and hemp), natural cosmetics and gifts, (including some made from recycled glass, paper and leather). The store includes a bookshop, a café and an entire floor dedicated to workshops and therapy treatments, including yoga, tai chi and shiatsu. You can even learn to play the didgeridoo here.

FASHION

Bargains

There are often excellent bargains to be found in Amsterdam, especially during the January and July sales. Watch for signs saying *Uitverkoop* (closing-down or end-of-season sale), *Solden* (sale) and *Korting* (discounted goods).

CANDY CORSON

One of the best places in Amsterdam for quality leather accessories, especially bags and belts.
⊞ H5 ⊠ St Luciensteeg 19 ☎ 6248061 🚃 Tram 13, 14, 17, 20

CORA KEMPERMAN

Elegant and imaginative, individually designed women's fashion.
⊞ G5 ⊠ Leidsestraat 72 ☎ 6251284 🚃 Tram 1, 2, 5

ESPRIT

Young, trendy designs for the seriously fashionable.
⊞ H5 ⊠ Spui 10a ☎ 6221967 🚃 Tram 1, 2, 5

HESTER VAN EEGHEN

Handbags, wallets and other leather accessories in innovative shapes, styles and colours, designed in Holland and made in Italy.
⊞ G5 ⊠ Hartenstraat 1 ☎ 6269212 🚃 Tram 13, 14, 17, 20

DE KNOPEN WINKEL

With 8,000 different kinds of buttons, from around the world, the Button Shop is on hand for apparel emergencies.
⊞ G5 ⊠ Wolvenstraat 14 ☎ 6240479 🚃 Tram 1, 2, 5

THE MADHATTER

Hand-made hats by Dutch designers.
⊞ H7 ⊠ Van der Helstplein 4 ☎ 6647748 🚃 Tram 3, 12, 25

MEXX

Top designer boutique where you'll find many leading French and Italian labels.
⊞ G6 ⊠ P C Hooftstraat 118 ☎ 6750171 🚃 Tram 2, 3, 5, 12, 20

OGER

One of the top menswear boutiques.
⊞ G6 ⊠ P C Hooftstraat 81 ☎ 6768695 🚃 Tram 2, 3, 5, 12, 20

OILILY

Children love the brightly coloured and patterned sporty clothes of this Dutch company.
⊞ G6 ⊠ P C Hooftstraat 131–133 ☎ 6723361 🚃 Tram 2, 3, 5, 12, 20

OSCAR

All the latest footwear here, from glittery platforms to psychedelic thigh boots.
⊞ H4 ⊠ Nieuwendijk 208–10 ☎ 6253143 🚃 Tram 4, 9, 14, 16, 20, 24, 25

PALETTE

The smallest shop in the Netherlands has a large selection of silk and satin shoes, in 500 colours.
⊞ H5 ⊠ Nieuwezijds Voorburgwal 125 ☎ 6393207 🚃 Tram 4, 9, 14, 16, 20, 24, 25

RETRO

Way-out fashion, including a dazzling array of '60s and '70s flower-power clothing.
⊞ F6 ⊠ 1e Constantijn Huygenstraat 57 ☎ 6834180 🚃 Tram 1, 3, 6, 12

SISSY-BOY

A Dutch clothing chain with stylish, affordable clothing for men and women.
⊞ G5 ⊠ Leidsestraat 15 ☎ 6238949 🚃 Tram 1, 2, 5

THEATRE, DANCE & FILM

THEATRE & DANCE

FELIX MERITIS

An important avant-garde dance and drama centre, and home to the Shaffy experimental theatre company.

🕂 G5 ✉ Keizersgracht 324 ☎ 6262321 🚋 Tram 13, 14, 17, 20

DE KLEINE KOMEDIE

The very best cabaret and stand-up comedy, in one of Amsterdam's oldest theatres.

🕂 H5 ✉ Amstel 56 ☎ 6240534 🚋 Tram 4, 9, 14, 20

KONINKLIJK THEATER CARRÉ

The 'Royal Theatre' plays host to long-running international musicals, revues, cabaret, folk dancing, and an annual Christmas circus.

🕂 H–J6 ✉ Amstel 115–25 ☎ 6225225 🚇 Weesperplein

MUZIEKTHEATER

An Amsterdam cultural mainstay and home to the Dutch national opera and ballet companies since it opened in 1986, Holland's largest auditorium, seating 1,689, mounts an international repertoire as well as experimental works. Guided backstage tours on Wed and Sat at 3PM (➤ 55).

🕂 H5 ✉ Waterlooplein 22 ☎ 6255455 (recorded information in Dutch; hold for operator) 🚇 Waterlooplein

STADSSCHOUWBURG

Classical and modern plays form the main repertoire of the stylish, 19th-century Municipal Theatre.

🕂 G6 ✉ Leidseplein 26 ☎ 6242311 🚋 Tram 1, 2, 5, 6, 7, 10, 20

DE STALHOUDERIJ

One of the city's very few English-language theatre companies, in a converted stable that seats 40.

🕂 G5 ✉ 1e Bloemdwarsstraat 4 ☎ 6262282 🚋 Tram 13, 14, 17, 20

VONDELPARK OPENLUCHTTHEATER

The open-air theatre in the park offers drama, cabaret, concerts and children's programmes from June to August.

🕂 F6 ✉ Vondelpark ☎ 5237700 🚋 Tram 1, 2, 3, 5, 6, 12, 20

FILM

CITY 1–7

Amsterdam's largest multi-screen cinema.

🕂 G6 ✉ Kleine Gartmanplantsoen 13–25 ☎ 6234579 🚋 Tram 1, 2, 5, 6, 7, 10, 20

FILM MUSEUM CINEMATHEEK

International programmes, ranging from silent movies to more recent releases.

🕂 G6 ✉ Vondelpark 3 ☎ 5891400 🚋 Tram 1, 2, 3, 5, 6, 12, 20

TUCHINSKI THEATER

Holland's most attractive and prestigious cinema, with six screens; classic art deco interior alone makes it worth visiting, no matter what's showing.

🕂 H5 ✉ Reguliersbreestraat 26–28 ☎ 6262633 🚋 Tram 4, 9, 14, 20

Tickets

For theatre information and tickets, contact the Amsterdam Uit Buro's Ticketshop (✉ Leidseplein 26 ☎ 6211211 🕓 office open daily 10–6, Thu until 9; telephone answered 9–9 daily). Tickets for most performances can also be purchased from the VVV tourist offices. The daily newspapers and listings magazine *Uitkrant* have programme details.

Film guide

The city's main multi-screen cinema complexes, in the Leidseplein and Rembrandtplein areas, follow Hollywood's lead closely. The latest big US releases and British films that become international hits are sure to show up on Amsterdam's screens after a short delay. Films from other countries occasionally make it to the screen.

Almost all films are shown in their original language, with Dutch subtitles.

CLASSICAL MUSIC & OPERA

BEURS VAN BERLAGE

Home to the Netherlands Philharmonic Orchestra and Dutch Chamber Orchestra, this remarkable early modernist building that once housed the stock exchange now makes an impressive concert hall (➤ 54).

➕ H4–5 ✉ Damrak 213–279 ☎ 6270466
🚊 Tram 4, 9, 16, 20, 24, 25

CONCERTGEBOUW

One of the world's finest concert halls, the magnificent neoclassical Concertgebouw has wonderful acoustics, making it a favourite with musicians worldwide. Since the Royal Concertgebouw Orchestra made its début in 1888, it has come under the baton of Richard Strauss, Mahler, Ravel, Schönberg and Haitink to name but a few. It continues to be one of the most respected ensembles in the world.

➕ G7 ✉ Concertgebouwplein 2–6 ☎ 6718345 🚊 Tram 3, 5, 12, 16, 20

IJSBREKER

A major international venue for contemporary classical music. There are performances of work by John Cage, Xanakis and other modern music pioneers, and around half the concerts are devoted to modern Dutch compositions.

➕ J6 ✉ Weesperzijde 23 ☎ 6939093 🚇 Weesperplein

MUZIEKTHEATER

Major operatic works and experimental opera from the Dutch National

Opera and other leading international companies (➤ 55 and 77).

➕ H5 ✉ Waterlooplein 22 ☎ 6255455 🚇 Waterlooplein

NIEUWE KERK

Frequent lunchtime concerts and exceptional organ recitals by visiting organists, in an atmospheric setting (➤ 37).

➕ H5 ✉ Dam ☎ 6268168 🚊 Tram 1, 2, 4, 5, 9, 13, 14, 16, 17, 20, 24, 25

OUDE KERK

Chamber music concerts and organ recitals are held in this old church, where Holland's foremost composer, Jan Pieters Sweelinck (1562–1621) was once organist. Pass by at 4PM on Saturdays, and you may hear a carillon concert (➤ 40).

➕ H5 ✉ Oudekerksplein 23 ☎ 6258284 🚇 Nieuwmarkt

RAI

This convention centre sometimes stages classical music and opera.

➕ G–H8 ✉ Europaplein ☎ 5491212 🚊 Tram 4

TROPENMUSEUM

Traditional music from developing countries is performed at the museum's Soeterijn Theatre (➤ 48).

➕ K6 ✉ Linnaeusstraat 2 ☎ 5688215 🚊 Tram 6, 9, 10, 14, 20

WESTERGASFABRIEK

A popular venue for experimental opera.

➕ F3 ✉ Haarlemmerweg 8–10 ☎ 5810425 🚌 Bus 18 Tram 10

Ticket time

For performances at popular venues, including the Concertgebouw and Muziektheater, you generally need to book ahead. This can be done in person or by phone to ticket reservation counters. VVV tourist offices also book tickets for a small charge, as does Amsterdam Uit Buro's Ticketshop (✉ Leidseplein 26 ☎ 6211211). Many hotels can reserve tickets for guests.

LIVE MUSIC

AKHNATON
Funky multi-cultural youth centre with reggae, rap and salsa dance nights.
✚ H4 ✉ Nieuwezijds Kolk 25 ☎ 6243396 🚊 Tram 1, 2, 5, 13, 17, 20

ALTO JAZZ CAFÉ
One of Amsterdam's best jazz clubs. Live music nightly, pricey drinks.
✚ G6 ✉ Korte Leidsedwarsstraat 115 ☎ 6263249 🚊 Tram 1, 2, 5, 6, 7, 10, 20

BIMHUIS
The place for serious followers of avant-garde, improvisational and experimental jazz, attracting top international players.
✚ H5 ✉ Oudeschans 73–77 ☎ 6231361 Ⓜ Nieuwmarkt

BOURBON STREET
Nightly blues and jazz.
✚ G6 ✉ Leidsekruisstraat 6–8 ☎ 6233440 🚊 Tram 6, 7, 10, 20

CANEÇAO
Brazilian bar with live salsa nightly.
✚ G6 ✉ Lange Leidsedwarsstraat 86 ☎ 6380611 🚊 Tram 1, 2, 5, 6, 7, 10, 20

DE HEEREN VAN AEMSTEL
Prior to events such as the North Sea Jazz Festival, you can often see some of the world's great jazz performers here.
✚ H6 ✉ Thorbeckeplein 5 ☎ 6202173 🚊 Tram 4, 9, 14, 20

HOF VAN HOLLAND
Come here for an evening of Dutch folk music and traditional songs.
✚ H5 ✉ Rembrandtplein 5 ☎ 6234650 🚊 Tram 4, 9, 14, 20

JOSEPH LAM JAZZ CAFÉ
Traditional jazz club with live Dixieland on Saturdays.
✚ G3 ✉ Van Diemenstraat 242 ☎ 6228086 🚌 Bus 28

MALOE MELO
This smoky yet convivial Jordaan bar, Amsterdam's 'home of the blues', belts out some fine rhythms.
✚ G4 ✉ Lijnbaansgracht 163 ☎ 4204592 🚊 Tram 3, 10

O'REILLY'S IRISH PUB
Choice whiskeys and hearty Irish fare accompanied by jolly folk music.
✚ H5 ✉ Paleisstraat 103–105 ☎ 6249498 🚊 Tram 1, 2, 5

PARADISO
Rock, reggae and pop concerts, in a beautiful old converted church that was once the haunt of '60s hippies. Now the discotheque offers music from the 1970s to the latest dance trends.
✚ G6 ✉ Weteringschans 6–8 ☎ 6237348 🚊 Tram 6, 7, 10

TWEE ZWAANTJES
Traditional Dutch entertainment off the tourist track in a tiny bar full of accordion-playing, folk-singing Jordaaners.
✚ G4 ✉ Prinsengracht 114 ☎ 6252729 🚊 Tram 13, 14, 17, 20

Melkweg
Located in a wonderful old dairy building (hence the name *Melkweg* or 'Milky Way') on a canal just off Leidseplein, this off-beat arts centre opened in the '60s and remains a shrine to alternative culture. Live bands play in the old warehouse most evenings, and there is also a constantly changing programme of unconventional theatre, dance, art and film events.
(✉ Lijnbaansgracht 234 ☎ 6248492).

79

BROWN CAFÉS & OTHER BARS

Ancient and modern

Brown cafés, so-called because of their chocolate-coloured walls and dark wooden fittings, are reminiscent of the interiors in Dutch Old Master paintings. Here you can meet the locals in a setting that's *gezellig* (cosy). In stark contrast, there are a growing number of brasserie-like grand cafés, and chic, modern bars, with stylish, spacious interiors. Look out also for the tiny ancient *proeflokalen* tasting bars (originally distillers' private sampling rooms), with ageing barrels and gleaming brass taps, serving a host of gins and liqueurs.

BROWN CAFÉS

FRASCATI

A lively, cultured crowd frequent this bar next to an experimental theatre.
⊞ H5 ⊠ Nes 59 ☎ 6241324
🚋 Tram 4, 9, 14, 16, 20, 24, 25

HOPPE

One of Amsterdam's most established, most popular brown cafés, with beer in one bar and gin from the barrel in another.
⊞ G5 ⊠ Spui 18–20
☎ 4204420 🚋 Tram 1, 2, 5

DE KARPERSHOEK

A sawdust-strewn bar dating from 1629, and frequented by sailors.
⊞ H4 ⊠ Martelaarsgracht 2
☎ 6247886 🚉 Centraal Station

HET MOLENPAD

An old-fashioned brown café. The canalside terrace catches the early evening sun.
⊞ G5 ⊠ Prinsengracht 653
☎ 6259680 🚋 Tram 1, 2, 5

PAPENEILAND

Amsterdam's oldest bar resembles a scene from a Dutch Old Master painting, with its panelled walls, Makkum tiles, candles, benches and wood-burning stove.
⊞ G4 ⊠ Prinsengracht 2
☎ 6241989 🚌 Bus 18, 22

DE PRINS

Very much a locals' bar, despite its proximity to the Anne Frankhuis, with a cosy pub atmosphere and seasonal menu.
⊞ G4 ⊠ Prinsengracht 124
☎ 6249382 🚋 Tram 13, 14, 17, 20

VAN PUFFELEN

An intimate sawdust-strewn brown bar with a smart restaurant in the back. You can sit on a barge moored outside, on the Prinsengracht, in summer.
⊞ G5 ⊠ Prinsengracht 375–377 ☎ 6246270
🚋 Tram 13, 14, 17, 20

REIJNDERS

Brown cafés are typically on tranquil streets; Reijnders is on brash, neon-lit Leidseplein yet has retained much of its traditional style and look.
⊞ G6 ⊠ Leidseplein 6
☎ 6234419 🚋 Tram 1, 2, 5, 6, 7, 10, 20

GRAND CAFÉS & STYLISH BARS

DE ENGELBEWAARDER

Jazz on Sunday from 4PM livens up a usually tranquil, arty hangout situated off the Red Light District.
⊞ H5 ⊠ Kloveniersburgwal 59
☎ 6253772
🚇 Nieuwmarkt

DE JAREN

A spacious, ultra-modern café, known for its trendy clientele and its sunny terraces overlooking the Amstel.
⊞ H5 ⊠ Nieuwe Doelenstraat 20–22 ☎ 6255771
🚋 Tram 4, 9, 14, 16, 20, 24, 25

DE KROON

A chic, colonial-style bar with large potted plants and wicker furniture, and an executive clientele.
⊞ H5 ⊠ Rembrandtplein 17
☎ 6252011 🚋 Tram 4, 9, 14, 20

HET LAND VAN WALEM

One of Amsterdam's first modern bars.

✚ G5 ✉ Keizersgracht 449
☎ 6253544 🚊 Tram 1, 2, 5

LUXEMBOURG

Watch the world go by over canapés or colossal club sandwiches on the terrace of this elegant, high-ceilinged bar.

✚ G5 ✉ Spui 22–24
☎ 6206264 🚊 Tram 1, 2, 5

L'OPERA

Fashionable with the city's chic set.

✚ H5 ✉ Rembrandtplein 27–31 ☎ 6275232
🚊 Tram 4, 9, 14, 20

SCHILLER

An evocative art deco bar enhanced with live piano music.

✚ H5 ✉ Rembrandtplein 26
☎ 6249846 🚊 Tram 4, 9, 14, 20

PROEFLOKALEN (TASTING BARS)

CAFÉ HOOGHOUDT

Brown bar-cum-*proeflokalen* in an old warehouse lined with traditional stoneware *jenever* barrels. Tasty Dutch appetisers go with a big selection of liqueurs.

✚ H6 ✉ Reguliersgracht 11
☎ 4204041 🕐 Noon–1AM
🚊 Tram 4, 9, 14, 16, 20, 24, 25

DE DRIE FLESCHJES

Amsterdammers have been tasting gins at 'The Three Little Bottles' since 1650.

✚ H5 ✉ Gravenstraat 18
☎ 6248443 🚊 Tram 1, 2, 4, 5, 9, 13, 14, 16, 17, 20, 24, 25

DE OOIEVAAR

A homely atmosphere pervades 'The Stork', one of Holland's smallest *proeflokalen*.

✚ H4 ✉ Sint Olofspoort 1
☎ 4208004 🚉 Centraal Station

SPECIALIST BARS

DE BEIAARD

A beer drinker's paradise – over 80 beers from around the world.

✚ G5 ✉ Spui 30
☎ 6225110 🚊 Tram 1, 2, 5

BROUWERIJ 'T IJ

Lethally strong beer brewed on the premises of the old De Gooier windmill (► 60).

✚ K5 ✉ Funenkade 7
☎ 6228325 🕐 Fri–Sun 3PM–8PM 🚌 Bus 22, 28

BULLDOG PALACE

Flagship of the Bulldog chain of bars and smoking coffee shops – a plush, loud bar, brashly decked out in stars and stripes. Downstairs is a 'smoking coffee shop' (► 69).

✚ G6 ✉ Leidseplein 13–17
☎ 6271908 🚊 Tram 1, 2, 5, 6, 7, 10, 20

CYBER C@FÉ

The first of several internet cafés in Amsterdam.

✚ H4 ✉ Nieuwendijk 19
☎ 6235146 (e-mail: visitor1@cybercafe.euronet.nl)
🚉 Centraal Station

CAFÉ APRIL

Popular, easy-going gay bar that attracts a mixed crowd of mostly male locals and tourists.

✚ H5 ✉ Reguliersdwarsstraat 37 ☎ 6259572 🚊 Tram 1, 2, 5

Bar talk

Most of the 1,400 bars and cafés in Amsterdam are open from around 10AM until the early hours and many serve meals. *Proeflokalen* open from around 4PM until 8PM, and some serve snacks, such as nuts, cheese, meatballs and sausage. Beer is the most popular alcoholic drink. It is always served with a head, and often with a *jenever* chaser called a *kopstoot* (a blow to the head). If you want only a small beer, ask for a *colatje* or *Kleintje pils*. Dutch for 'cheers' is *Proost!*

Jenevers

Dutch gin (*jenever*), made from molasses and flavoured with juniper berries, comes in a variety of ages: *jong* (young), *oud* (old) and *zeer oud* (the oldest and the mellowest), and in colour ranging from clear to brownish. Other flavours may be added; try *bessenjenever* (blackcurrant), or *bitterkoekjes likeur* (macaroon). *Jenever* is drunk straight or as a beer chaser, not with a mixer.

NIGHTCLUBS

Gay Amsterdam

Clubbing is at the heart of Amsterdam's gay scene. The best-known venue is iT, a glitzy disco with throbbing techno. Gay bars and clubs abound in nearby Reguliersdwarsstraat and Halvemaansteeg. To find out exactly what's on and where it's happening, call the Gay and Lesbian Switchboard (☎ 6236565) or read the English-language *Guide for Gays* magazine.

BOSTON CLUB

Attracts a 30s–40s crowd looking for a quieter dancing experience.
✚ H4 ✉ Renaissance Hotel, Kattengat 1 ☎ 6245561 or 6275245 (hotel) 🚊 Centraal Station

DANSEN BIJ JANSEN

Student disco, playing the latest chart toppers.
✚ H5 ✉ Handboogstraat 11 ☎ 6201779 🕐 11PM–4:30AM 🚊 Tram 1, 2, 5,

ESCAPE

Amsterdam's largest disco can hold 2,000 dancers. Dazzling light show, superb sound system.
✚ H5 ✉ Rembrandtplein 11–15 ☎ 6221111 🕐 10PM–4AM (Fri, Sat until 5AM) 🚊 Tram 4, 9, 14, 20

HOLLAND CASINO

One of Europe's largest casinos.
✚ G6 ✉ Max Euweplein 62 ☎ 5211111 🚊 Tram 1, 2, 5, 6, 7, 10, 20

iT

The wildest disco in town, with outrageously dressed clientele and fierce house music. Saturday night is exclusively gay.
✚ H5 ✉ Amstelstraat 24 ☎ 6250111 🕐 11PM–4AM. Closed Sun–Wed 🚊 Tram 4, 9, 14, 20

MAZZO

A young image-conscious crowd prop up the bar of this small, trendy disco in the Jordaan, where guest DJs and live bands play the latest sounds.
✚ G5 ✉ Rozengracht 114 ☎ 6267500 🕐 11PM–4AM (Sat 5AM) 🚊 Tram 13, 14, 17, 20

MINISTRY

A café-cum-nightclub with all kinds of disco music.
✚ H5 ✉ Reguliersdwarsstraat 12 ☎ 6233981 🕐 Thu–Mon 10–5 🚊 Tram 1, 2, 5, 16, 20, 24, 25

ODEON

A converted canal house with house music on the first floor, '60s–'80s classic disco upstairs, and jazz in the basement.
✚ H5 ✉ Singel 460 ☎ 6249711 🕐 10PM–4AM (Fri, Sat until 5AM) 🚊 Tram 1, 2, 5

RICHTER

The '36 on the Richter Scale' club with 'earth-quake' décor is enchanting.
✚ H5 ✉ Reguliersdwarsstraat 36 ☎ 6261573 🕐 midnight–4:30AM 🚊 Tram 1, 2, 5, 16, 20, 24, 25

RoXY

Set in an old cinema, this cool club is a favourite with Amsterdam's chic club-set.
✚ H5 ✉ Singel 465–467 ☎ 6200354 🕐 11PM–4AM (Fri, Sat until 5AM) 🚊 Tram 1, 2, 4, 5, 9, 14, 20, 24, 25

SALAD BOWL

Jazz dance, soul, disco and hip-hop in trendy surroundings.
✚ H5 ✉ Nieuwezijds Voorburgwal 161 ☎ 4205062 🚊 Tram 1, 2, 5, 13, 17, 20

SOUL KITCHEN

Leading 'non-house' club for soul and also '60s and '70s music.
✚ H5 ✉ Amstelstraat 32 ☎ 6202333 🕐 Wed–Mon 11PM–5AM 🚊 Tram 4, 9, 14, 20

SPORTS

FISHING

Obtain a permit from the Dutch Fishing Federation to fish in the Amsterdamse Bos (► 58).

✚ H6 ✉ Nicolaas Witsenstraat 10 ☎ 6264988 🚃 Tram 6, 7, 10

FITNESS
JANSEN AEROBIC FITNESSCENTRUM

Fitness centre with gyms, sauna, solarium and daily aerobics classes.

✚ H5 ✉ Rokin 109–111 ☎ 6269366 🚃 Tram 4, 9, 14, 16, 20, 24, 25

GOLF
GOLFBAAN WATERLAND

Modern 18-hole course just north of the city centre.

✚ L1 ✉ Buikslotermeerdijk 141 ☎ 6361010

HORSE RIDING
HOLLANDSCHE MANEGE

Amsterdam's most central riding school dating from 1882.

✚ F6 ✉ Vondelstraat 140 ☎ 6180942 🚃 Tram 1, 6

JOGGING

There are marked trails for joggers through the Vondelpark and Amsterdamse Bos. The Amsterdam Marathon is in May, and the Grachtenloop canal race in June (► 22), when up to 5,000 run either 5, 10, or 20km along the banks of Prinsengracht and Vijzelgracht.

ICE SKATING

The canals often freeze in winter, turning the city into a big ice rink. Skates can be bought at most sports equipment shops.

JAAP EDENBAAN

A large indoor ice rink, open October to March.

✚ L7 ✉ Radioweg 64 ☎ 6949652 🚃 Tram 9

SWIMMING

The seaside is only 30 minutes away by train, with miles of clean, sandy beaches. Zandvoort is closest; Bergen and Noordwijk are also popular.

MARNIXBAD

A normal, rectangular indoor swimming pool, but with the addition of water slides and whirlpool.

✚ G4 ✉ Marnixplein 5 ☎ 6254843 🚃 Tram 3, 10

DE MIRANDABAD

Sub-tropical swimming pool complex, with indoor and outdoor pools, beach and wave machines.

✚ H8 ✉ De Mirandalaan 9 ☎ 6428080 🚃 Tram 25

TENNIS
AMSTELPARK TENNIS CENTRE

Holland's biggest, with 42 outdoor and indoor courts, the outdoor ones floodlit, and all open to visitors.

✚ F9 ✉ Koenenkade 8, Amsterdamse Bos ☎ 6445436 🚌 Bus 125, 147, 170, 171, 172, 193

WATERSPORTS
DUIKELAAR, SLOTERPARK

A water park with sail boats, canoes and sailboards to rent in summer.

✚ C5 ✉ Noordzijde 41 ☎ 6138855 🚃 Tram 14

Spectator sports

Soccer is Holland's number one spectator sport and the number one team is Ajax Amsterdam. Watch them play at their magnificent new stadium, the Amsterdam ArenA, ArenaBoulevard, Amsterdam Zuidoost (☎ 3111333). Other popular events include international field hockey at Wagenaar Stadium (✉ Nieuwe Kalfjeslaan ☎ 6401141) and equestrian show-jumping at RAI (✉ Europaplein ☎ 5491212) every November. Look out for a Dutch hybrid of volleyball and netball called *korfball*, and *carambole* – billiards on a table without pockets.

LUXURY HOTELS

Prices

Expect to pay over f400 a night for a double room in a luxury hotel.

Hotel tips

Two-fifths of Amsterdam's 30,000 hotel beds are in 4- and 5-star properties, making problems for people looking for mid-range and budget accommodation. At peak times, such as during the spring tulip season and summer, empty rooms in lower-cost hotels are about as rare as black tulips. Book ahead for these times. Special offers may be available at other times. Many hotels lower their rates in winter, when the city is quieter and truer to itself than in the mad whirl of summer. Watch out for hidden pitfalls, such as Golden Age canal houses with four floors, steep and narrow stairways and no lift; and tranquil-looking mansions with a late-night café's pavement terrace next door.

AMERICAN
Resplendent art-nouveau Amsterdam classic on the Leidseplein.
✚ G6 ✉ Leidsekade 97 ☎ 6245322 🚋 Tram 1, 2, 5, 6, 7, 10, 20

AMSTEL INTER-CONTINENTAL
Holland's most luxurious and expensive hotel, on the Amstel river, notable for its stately grandeur and opulent decor, is a little way from the centre, but provides a motor yacht and luxury limousines to make sightseeing easier.
✚ J6 ✉ Prof Tulpplein 1 ☎ 6226060 🚋 Tram 6, 7, 10, 20

BILDERBERG GARDEN
In a pleasant leafy suburb, a short tram ride from the city centre.
✚ F7 ✉ Dijsselhofplantsoen 7 ☎ 6642121 🚋 Tram 16

DE L'EUROPE
Prestigious, combining late-Victorian architecture with the most modern amenities, in a waterfront setting.
✚ H5 ✉ Nieuwe Doelenstraat 2–8 ☎ 5311777 🚋 Tram 4, 6, 9, 14, 16, 20, 24, 25

GOLDEN TULIP BARBIZON PALACE
Modern luxury deftly concealed within a row of 17th-century mansions. Many split-level suites with ancient oak beams.
✚ H4 ✉ Prins Hendrikkade 59–72 ☎ 5564564 🚉 Centraal Station

GRAND HOTEL KRASNAPOLSKY
Built in the 1880s, the 'Kras' has belle-époque grace in its public spaces and modern facilities in its rooms.
✚ H5 ✉ Dam 9 ☎ 5549111 🚋 Tram 1, 2, 4, 5, 9, 13, 14, 16, 17, 20, 24, 25

GRAND WESTIN DEMEURE
Once a 16th-century royal inn, then the City Hall, now a luxury hotel.
✚ H5 ✉ Oudezijds Voorburgwal 197 ☎ 5553111 🚉 Nieuwmarkt

HILTON
Modern efficiency, on a leafy boulevard in the south of the city. The honeymoon suite was the scene of John Lennon and Yoko Ono's week-long 1969 'love-in' for world peace.
✚ F7 ✉ Apollolaan 138–140 ☎ 6780780 🚋 Tram 16

MARRIOTT
An easy walk to the main museums, shops and nightlife centres.
✚ G6 ✉ Stadhouderskade 19–21 ☎ 6075555 🚋 Tram 1, 2, 5, 6, 20

PULITZER
Twenty-four 17th-century houses, once the homes of wealthy merchants, have been converted into this luxurious canalside hotel.
✚ G5 ✉ Prinsengracht 315–331 ☎ 5235235 🚋 Tram 13, 14, 17, 20

RENAISSANCE
Modern, with extensive business facilities and own disco, near Dam square and Centraal Station.
✚ H4 ✉ Kattengat 1 ☎ 6212223 🚋 Tram 1, 2, 5, 17, 20

MID-RANGE HOTELS

AMBASSADE
Amsterdam's smartest B&B, in a series of gabled canal houses.
✚ G5 ✉ Herengracht 335–353 ☎ 6262333 🚊 Tram 1, 2, 5

AMSTERDAM
Fully modernised behind its 18th-century façade, on one of the city's busiest tourist streets.
✚ H5 ✉ Damrak 93–94 ☎ 5550666 🚊 Tram 4, 9, 14, 16, 20, 24, 25

AMSTERDAM HOUSE
Quietly situated small hotel beside the Amstel. Most rooms have a view of the river.
✚ H5 ✉ 's-Gravelandseveer 3–4 ☎ 6246607 🚊 Tram 4, 9, 14, 16, 20, 24, 25

CANAL HOUSE
Antique furnishings and a pretty garden make this small, family-run hotel on the Keizersgracht a gem.
✚ G4 ✉ Keizersgracht 148 ☎ 6225182 🚊 Tram 13, 14, 17, 20

LA CASALO
A converted houseboat with just four rooms.
✚ J7 ✉ Amsteldijk 862 ☎ 6423680 🚊 Tram 4

DOELEN HOTEL
Amsterdam's oldest hotel, the place where Rembrandt painted the 'Night Watch', with small rooms, but well-equipped.
✚ H5 ✉ Nieuwe Doelenstraat 24 ☎ 5540600 🚊 Tram 4, 9, 14, 16, 20, 24, 25

ESTHERÉA
A well-considered blend of wood-panelled canalside character with efficient service and modern facilities.
✚ G5 ✉ Singel 303–309 ☎ 6245146 🚊 Tram 1, 2, 5

JAN LUYKEN
A well-run, elegant town house hotel in a quiet back street near Vondelpark and the Museumplein.
✚ G6 ✉ Jan Luijkenstraat 54–58 ☎ 5730730 🚊 Tram 2, 3, 5, 12

MAAS
A charming, family-run, waterfront hotel round the corner from Leidseplein, near museums, shops and nightlife. Some rooms have waterbeds.
✚ G6 ✉ Leidsekade 91 ☎ 6233868 🚊 Tram 1, 2, 5, 6, 7, 10, 20

REMBRANDT RESIDENCE
On Amsterdam's most celebrated canal.
✚ G5 ✉ Herengracht 255 ☎ 6236638 🚊 Tram 13, 14, 17, 20

SEVEN BRIDGES
Small and exquisite, with a view of seven bridges, lots of antiques, and owners who treat their guests as though they were family friends.
✚ H6 ✉ Reguliersgracht 31 ☎ 6231329 🚊 Tram 16, 24, 25

TULIP INN
Strikingly modern Amsterdam School-style architecture. Good facilities for visitors with disabilities.
✚ G5 ✉ Spuistraat 288–292 ☎ 4204545 🚊 Tram 1, 2, 5

Prices
Expect to pay from f200 to f400 a night for a double room in a mid-range hotel.

Bed and breakfast, apartments and boats
If you want to rent an apartment in Amsterdam, contact Amsterdam House (✉ Amstel 176a ☎ 6262577); you can take your pick of luxury apartments in converted canal houses, or even a houseboat. Bed and Breakfast Holland (✉ Theophile de Bockstraat 3, ☎ 6157527) will set you up in a private house.

BUDGET ACCOMMODATION

Prices

Expect to pay up to f200 a night for a double room in a budget hotel. Hostels and campsites are considerably cheaper.

Camping

There are several campsites in and around Amsterdam. The best-equipped one is a long way out, in the Amsterdamse Bos (✉ Kleine Noorddijk 1, ☎ 6416868). Vliegenbos is just a ten-minute bus ride from the station, close to the River IJ (✉ Meeuwenlaan 138, ☎ 6368855). Contact the VVV for full details.

ACACIA

An inexpensive, cheerful, family-run hotel in the Jordaan, with self-catering studios and a houseboat that sleeps four.

✚ G4 ✉ Lindengracht 251 ☎ 6221460 🚋 Tram 3

AGORA

A small, comfortable, 18th-century canal house furnished with antiques and filled with flowers from the nearby Bloemenmarkt.

✚ H5 ✉ Singel 462 ☎ 6272200 🚋 Tram 4, 9, 14, 16, 20, 24, 25

AMSTEL BOTEL

One of Amsterdam's few floating hotels, with magnificent views over the old docks.

✚ J4 ✉ Oosterdokskade 2–4 ☎ 6264247 🚉 Centraal Station

ARENA

A large hostel and information centre for youthful travellers. It has a café and restaurant (with garden terrace), and puts on dance nights, concerts, exhibitions and other events.

✚ J6 ✉ 's-Gravesandestraat 51 ☎ 6947444 🚋 Tram 3, 6, 10

DE FILOSOOF

Each room in this unique hotel is named after the great philosophers and decorated accordingly.

✚ F6 ✉ Anna van den Vondelstraat 6 ☎ 6833013 🚋 Tram 1, 6

HOKSBERGEN

A basic hotel in an old canal house, an easy walk from the main city sights.

✚ G5 ✉ Singel 301 ☎ 6266043 🚋 Tram 1, 2, 5

NJHC CITY HOSTEL VONDELPARK

A wide range of modern options, from dormitories to family rooms.

✚ G6 ✉ Zandpad 5, Vondelpark ☎ 5898999 🚋 Tram 1, 2, 5, 6, 20

NOVA

A clean, simple, central hotel, with a friendly young staff.

✚ H5 ✉ Nieuwezijds Voorburgwal 272–276 ☎ 6230066 🚋 Tram 1, 2, 5

OWL

Family-owned hotel with bright, comfortable rooms and a garden, in a quiet street near Vondelpark.

✚ G6 ✉ Roemer Visscherstraat 1 ☎ 6189484 🚋 Tram 2, 3, 5, 12, 20

PRINSENHOF

Quaint, comfortable and clean. One of the city's best budget options.

✚ H6 ✉ Prinsengracht 810 ☎ 6231772 🚋 Tram 4

SINT-NICOLAAS

Rambling former factory and comfortable, if spare, facilities.

✚ H4 ✉ Spuistraat 1a ☎ 6261384 🚋 Tram 1, 2 ,5, 13, 17, 20

VAN OSTADE BICYCLE HOTEL

Small hotel that rents bikes and gives advice on how to discover hidden Amsterdam by bicycle.

✚ H7 ✉ Van Ostadestraat 123 ☎ 6793452 🚋 Tram 3, 12, 20, 24, 25

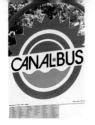

AMSTERDAM
travel facts

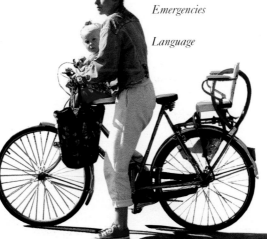

ARRIVING & DEPARTING

Before you go

- EU nationals and citizens of the USA, Canada, Australia and New Zealand need a valid passport or national identity card to stay for up to three months. Nationals of many other countries require a visa.
- For health advice obtain a Form E111 from a post office.

When to go

- Most tourists visit between April and September.
- From late March until late May is the time to see Holland's tulips in bloom.
- June, July and August are the sunniest months, but you can never be sure of good weather. Many people come in June for the Holland Festival.
- In winter, temperatures can drop so low that the canals freeze over.
- Christmas is always a busy tourist season.

Arriving by air

- Amsterdam has one international airport (Schiphol), 18km from the centre. Many international airlines operate scheduled and charter flights here, including British Airways, KLM uk, British Midlands, Aer Lingus, KLM, and Delta, Northwest (in alliance with Dutch national carrier KLM) and United Airlines from the US.
- Airport information ☎ 0900/0141.
- Trains leave the airport for Amsterdam Centraal Station every 15 minutes from 6AM until midnight, then hourly through the night. The ride takes 20 minutes and the one-way fare costs f6.25.
- A taxi from Schiphol Airport to the centre of Amsterdam costs around f70.

Arriving by sea and rail

- The major ferry ports, IJmuiden, Rotterdam and Hook of Holland, have good rail connections with Amsterdam. Regular sailings from the UK are offered by Stena Line, Scandinavian Seaways and P&O North Sea Ferries.
- There are good rail connections with most European cities.
- Train information ☎ 0900/9292.

Arriving by car

- Amsterdam is well served by motorways. From the A10 ring road, S-routes (indicated by blue signs) go into the city centre.
- In the centre, many streets are one-way, particularly in the canal area.
- Watch out for bicycles and trams.
- Street parking is very difficult in the centre. It is metered Monday to Saturday from 9AM to 11PM, Sunday noon to 11PM, and expensive (f2.75–4.75 per hour). Use parking lots instead.
- Always lock your car securely, and never leave valuables in it.

Customs regulations

- EU nationals are not required to declare items intended for personal use.
- For non-EU nationals the limits are:
  200 cigarettes or 50 cigars or 250g of tobacco
  1 litre spirits or 2 litres fortified wine or 2 litres non-sparkling wine
  50ml perfume, 500g coffee and 100g tea plus other goods to the value of f200.

Departing by air

- Airport tax is included in the price of your ticket.
- There are numerous duty-free shops at Schiphol Airport.

ESSENTIAL FACTS

Electricity
• 220 volts; round two-pin sockets.

Etiquette
• Shake hands on introduction. Once you know people better, you might exchange three pecks on alternate cheeks instead.
• Remember to say *hallo* and *dag* (goodbye) when shopping.
• Dress is generally informal, even for the opera, ballet and theatres.
• Although service charges are included in bills, tipping is customary. Round-off bills to the nearest guilder, or five guilders for larger bills.

Insurance
• Take out a comprehensive policy before you leave home.

Women travellers
• There are no particular risks for women travelling alone. For information and advice contact the Vrouwenhuis (Women's House) ✉ Nieuwe Herengracht 95 ☎ 6252066

Money matters
• The guilder (formerly called the florin) is abbreviated in numerous ways: f, fl, Hfl, Dfl, NLG. 1 guilder=100 cents.
• On 1 January 1999 the euro became the official currency of The Netherlands, and the Dutch guilder became a denomination of the euro. Dutch guilder notes and coins continue to be legal tender during a transitional period. Euro bank notes and coins are likely to start to be introduced by January 1 2002.
• Banks may offer a better exchange rate than hotels or independent bureaux de change. GWK offer 24-hour money-changing services at Schiphol Airport and Centraal Station.

National holidays
• 1 January; Good Friday, Easter Sunday and Monday; 30 April; Ascension Day; Pentecost and Pentecost Monday; 25 December and 26 December.
• 4 and 5 May – Remembrance Day (*Herdenkingsdag*) and Liberation Day (*Bevrijdingsdag*) – are World War II Commemoration Days but not public holidays.

Opening hours
• Banks: Mon–Fri 9 until 4 or 5. Some stay open Thu until 7.
• Shops: Tue–Sat 9 or 10 until 6, Mon 1 to 6. Some open Thu until 9 and Sun noon until 5. Some close early Sat, at 4 or 5.
• State-run museums and galleries: most open Tue–Sat 10 to 5, Sun and national holidays 1 to 5. Many close on Mon.

Places of worship
• Roman Catholic: Parish of the Blessed Trinity, Heilige Familie-kerk (✚ L8 ✉ Zouiersweg 180 ☎ 4652711)
• English Reformed Church: (✚ H5 ✉ Begijnhof 48 ☎ 6249665)
• Jewish: Jewish and Liberal Community Amsterdam: (✚ H9 ✉ Jacob Soetendorpstraat 8 ☎ 6423562)
• Muslim: THAIBA Islamic Cultural Centre: (✚ Off map ✉ Kraaiennest 125 ☎ 6982526)

Student travellers
• For discounts at some museums, galleries, theatres, restaurants and hotels, students under 26 can obtain an International Young Person's Passport (CJP – Cultureel Jongeren Passpoort), cost f20, from: AUB ✉ Leidseplein 26 ☎ 6211211; and NBBS ✉ Rokin 66 ☎ 6240989.

89

Time differences

- Amsterdam observes Central European Time, 1 hour ahead of Greenwich Mean Time in winter and 2 hours in summer.

Toilets

- There are few public toilets. Use the facilities in hotels, museums and cafés. There is often a small charge.

Tourist offices (VVV)

- The five main Vereniging Voor Vreemdelingenverkeer (VVV) offices all have multi-lingual staff, city maps and brochures. They will also make hotel, excursion, theatre and concert reservations for a small fee. They are:
  Centraal Station VVV
  (🚇 H4 ✉ Centraal Station, Platform 1)
  Stationsplein VVV
  (🚇 H4 ✉ Stationsplein 10)
  Leidseplein VVV
  (🚇 G6 ✉ Leidseplein 1)
  Stadionplein VVV
  (🚇 E8 ✉ Van Tuyll Van Serooskerkenweg 125)
  and Holland Tourism International at Schiphol Airport (🚇 Y12).
- For inquiries ☎ 0900/4004040.

Visitors with disabilities

- Facilities, especially in the hotels and museums along the canals, are not very good. Check in advance for facilities at tourist attractions, theatres and restaurants.
- VVV brochures include details of hotels and tourist attractions with access and facilities for people with disabilities.
- SGOA (Stichting Gehandicapten Overleg Amsterdam) provides information on suitable accommodation (🚇 G6 ✉ Quellijnstraat 84, 1072 ZA Amsterdam ☎ 020/5777955 ☎ 020/5777950 ☎ 020/5777960 📧 sgoa@xs4all.nl)
- There is a special taxi service for wheelchair users ☎ 6134134.

PUBLIC TRANSPORT

How to use the buses and trams

- The majority of buses and trams start from Centraal Station.
- Seventeen different tram lines run frequently from 6AM on weekdays (slightly later at weekends) until midnight when night buses take over, running hourly until 4AM. Day tickets are valid during the night following the day on which they are issued.
- If you need a ticket, board at the front and pay the driver.
- Take care when getting off. Many stops are in the middle of the road.

The Metro/light rail

- There are only three lines, all terminating at Centraal Station. They are used mainly by commuters from the suburbs. The most useful city-centre station is Nieuwmarkt.

Buying and using tickets

- The GVB (Transport Authority) network is divided into zones.
- The same ticket system is valid for tram, bus and Metro.
- If you intend to use public transport frequently, buy a ticket of 15 or 45 strips (*strippenkaart*), available at GVB and Dutch Railways ticket counters and the VVV. For each journey, a strip must be stamped for each zone you want to pass through, plus one for the journey: for example, from Centraal Station to Leidseplein is two zones, so you need to stamp two strips of your *strippenkaart*, plus one more. Zones are shown on maps at tram, bus and Metro stops.
- On buses: tell the driver the number of zones you want and your ticket will be stamped.
- On the Metro or light railway: before boarding, fold back the

appropriate number of strips and punch your ticket in the yellow ticket machines on the station.

- On trams: either ask the driver to stamp your ticket or do it yourself in a yellow punch-machine. Some trams have a conductor at the back who sells and stamps tickets.
- For a single trip, purchase a 'one-hour' ticket, from the driver of the bus or tram, or from a machine at the Metro entrance. Buy day and other tickets, 2-, 3-, 8-, 15-, and 45-strip cards from Metro and train station ticket counters, VVV offices, newsagents and bus/tram drivers.
- All tickets are valid for one hour after the time stamped on them, and include transfers.
- Don't travel without a valid ticket: you could be fined f60 plus the ticket price.
- For further information and maps, contact GVB (✚ H4 ✉ Stationsplein ☎ 0900/9292)

Getting around by bicycle

- Without doubt, the best way to see Amsterdam is by bicycle. To hire one costs from f12.50 a day, f60 a week.
  Damstraat Rent-a-Bike (✚ H5 Pieter Jacobszoondwarsstraat 11 ☎ 6255029 ◷ Daily 9–6)
  Bikes-a-Gogo (✚ G5 ✉ Elandsstraat 111 ☎ 6277726 ◷ Mon–Sat 9–6)

Taxis

- It is difficult to hail a taxi in the street. Go to a taxi stand outside major hotels, tourist attractions and Centraal Station. Fares are high, so add only a small tip.
- Taxicentrale (☎ 6777777) runs a reliable 24-hour service.
- Water taxis can be hailed, or ordered from the Water Taxi Centrale (✚ H4 ✉ Stationsplein 8 ☎ 6222181)

MEDIA & COMMUNICATIONS

Mail

- Postage to European destinations costs f1.60 for letters up to 20g, and f1 for postcards. Other destinations may be more.
- Purchase stamps (*postzegels*) at post offices, tobacco stores and souvenir shops.
- Post boxes are bright red and clearly marked 'ptt post'.

Post offices

- Most post offices open weekdays 8.30 or 9 until 5.
- Main Post Office: ✚ G5
  ✉ Hoofdpostkantoor PTT, Singel 250–256
  ☎ 5563311 ◷ Mon–Fri 9–6, Sat 9–1
- Postal Information: ☎ 0900/0417

Telephones

- Most public telephones take phonecards, costing f10, f25, or f50, available from telephone centres, post offices and railway stations.
- Phone calls within Europe cost about f1 per minute.
- Information: ☎ 0900/8008
- International information: ☎ 0900/0418
- Numbers starting 0900 are premium rate calls.
- Local and international operator: ☎ 0800/0410
- To phone abroad, dial 00 then the country code (UK 44, USA and Canada 1, Australia 61, New Zealand 64), then the number.
- Cheap rates: UK and Ireland 8AM–8PM and weekends; USA and Canada 7PM–10AM and weekends; Australia and New Zealand midnight–7AM, 3–8PM and weekends.
- Most hotels have International Direct Dialling, but it is expensive.
- At the Telecenter (✚ G5
  ✉ Raadhuisstraat 48), you can make

91

calls and pay afterwards with cash, credit card, traveller's cheque or Eurocheque.

Newspapers and magazines

- The main Dutch newspapers are *De Telegraaf* (right wing), *De Volkskrant* (left wing) and *NRC Handelsblad*.
- The main Amsterdam newspapers (sold nationwide) are *Het Parool* and *Nieuws van de Dag*.
- *Vrij Nederland* is a (very popular, left-wing) weekly news magazine.
- Listings magazines: *What's on in Amsterdam*, *Agenda* and *Uitkrant*.
- International newspapers are available at main kiosks, newsagents and bookshops.

Radio and television

- News is broadcast on Dutch Radio 1 (747kHz), classical music on Radio 4 (98.9mhz) and pop on Radio 3 (96.8mhz). BBC Radio 4 (long wave) is on 198kHzAM and the World Service (medium wave) is on 648kHzAM.
- There are five main Dutch TV channels and numerous cable and satellite stations, including BBC1 and 2, Sky, CNN and MTV.

EMERGENCIES

Emergency phone numbers

- Police: ☎ 112
- Ambulance: ☎ 112
- Fire Service: ☎ 112
- Tourist Medical Service: ☎ 6245793 (day), 5923355 (24hr)
- Automobile Emergency (ANWB): ☎ 0800/000888
- Lost credit cards: American Express ☎ 5048666, Diners Club ☎ 5573557, Master/Eurocard ☎ 030/2835555, Visa ☎ 6600611
- Sexual Abuse (◷ 24 hours): ☎ 6116022
- Crisis Helpline (◷ Mon–Thu 9AM–3AM, Fri–Sun 24 hours) ☎ 6757575

Embassies and consulates

- British Consulate: ✚ F7 ✉ Koningslaan 44 ☎ 6764343
- American Consulate: ✚ G6 ✉ Museumplein 19 ☎ 6645661
- Canadian Embassy: ✉ Sophianlaan 7, The Hague ☎ 070/3111600
- Australian Embassy: ✉ Carnegielean 4a, The Hague ☎ 070/3108200
- New Zealand Embassy: ✉ Carnegielaan 10, The Hague ☎ 070/3469324
- Irish Embassy: ✉ Dr. Kayperstraat 9, The Hague ☎ 070/3630993
- South African Embassy: ✉ Wassenaarseweg 40, The Hague ☎ 070/3924501

Lost Property

- For insurance purposes, report lost or stolen property to the police as soon as possible.
- Main lost property offices: Centraal Station (✚ H4 ✉ Stationsplein 15 ☎ 5578544 ◷ 7AM–11PM daily); Police Lost Property (✚ K7 ✉ Steffersonstraat ☎ 5593005 ◷ Mon–Fri noon–3.30)
- For property lost on public transport, GVB (✚ H4 ✉ Prins Hendrikkade 108–14 ☎ 5578544 ◷ Mon–Fri 9–4)

Medicines

- For non-prescription drugs, plasters and so on, go to a *drogist*.
- For prescription medicines, go to an *apotheek*, open Mon–Fri 8:30–5:30.
- Details of pharmacies open outside normal hours are in the daily newspaper *Het Parool* and all pharmacy windows.
- The Central Medical Service (☎ 020/5923434) can refer you to a duty GP or dentist.
- Hospital outpatient clinics are open 24 hours a day. The most central is Onze Lieve Vrouwe Gasthuis (✚ J6 ✉ 1e Oosterparkstraat 279 ☎ 5999111 ▣ Trams 3, 6, 10)

Precautions

- Pickpockets are common in busy shopping streets and markets, and in the Red Light District. Take sensible precautions and remain on your guard at all times.
- At night, avoid poorly lit areas and keep to busy streets. Amsterdam is not a dangerous city, but muggings do occur.

LANGUAGE

Basics

yes	ja
no	nee
please	alstublieft
thank you	dank u
hello	hallo
good morning	goedemorgen
good afternoon	goedemiddag
good evening	goedenavond
good night	welterusten
goodbye	dag
breakfast	het ontbijt

Useful words

good/bad	goed/slecht
big/small	groot/klein
hot/cold	warm/koud
new/old	nieuw/oud
open/closed	open/gesloten
push/pull	duwen/trekken
entrance/exit	ingang/uitgang
men's/women's	heren/damen
toilet	wc
free/occupied	vrij/bezet
far/near	ver/dichtbij
left/right	links/rechts
straight ahead	rechtdoor

Restaurant

breakfast	het ontbijt
lunch	de lunch
dinner	het diner
menu	de kaart
winelist	de wijnkaart
main course	het hoofdgerecht
dessert	het nagerecht
the bill, please	mag ik afrekenen

Numbers

1	een	15	vijftien
2	twee	16	zestien
3	drie	17	zeventien
4	vier	18	achtien
5	vijf	19	negentien
6	zes	20	twintig
7	zeven	21	eenentwintig
8	acht	22	tweeëntwintig
9	negen	30	dertig
10	tien	40	veertig
11	elf	50	vijftig
12	twaalf	100	honderd
13	dertien	1,000	duizend
14	veertien		

Days and times

Sunday	Zondag
Monday	Maandag
Tuesday	Dinsdag
Wednesday	Woensdag
Thursday	Donderdag
Friday	Vrijdag
Saturday	Zaterdag
today	vandaag
yesterday	gisteren
tomorrow	morgen

Useful phrases

Do you speak English? Spreekt u engels?

Do you have a vacant room? Zijn er nog kamers vrij?

with bath/shower met bad/douche

I don't understand Ik versta u niet

I'm sorry Sorry

Where is/are …? Waar is/zijn …?

How far is it to …? Hoe ver is het naar …?

How much does this cost? Hoeveel kost dit? …

Do you take (credit cards/traveller's checks)? Accepteert u (credit cards/reischeques)?

What time do you open? Hoe laat gaat u open?

What time do you close? How laat gaat u dicht?

Can you help me? Kunt u mij helpen?

INDEX

CityPack
Amsterdam

Written by   Teresa Fisher
Edited, designed and produced by
　　　　　　　 AA Publishing
Maps   © The Automobile Association 1997, 1999
Fold-out map © Falk-Verlag AG
　　　　　　　 © Kartographie GeoData

Distributed in the United Kingdom by AA Publishing.

The contents of this publication are believed correct at the time of printing. Nevertheless, the publishers cannot be held responsible for any errors or omissions or for changes in the details given in this guide or for the consequences of any reliance on the information provided by the same. Assessments of attractions, hotels, restaurants and so forth are based upon the author's own personal experience and, therefore, descriptions given in this guide necessarily contain an element of subjective opinion which may not reflect the publishers' opinion or dictate a reader's own experiences on another occasion.
We have tried to ensure accuracy in this guide, but things do change and we would be grateful if readers would advise us of any inaccuracies they may encounter.

© The Automobile Association 1997, 1999
First published 1997. Reprinted Jan, Mar, Oct, Dec 1998, Mar 1999.
Second edition 1999

A CIP catalogue record for this book is available from the British Library.

ISBN 0 7495 2215 1

Published by AA Publishing (a trading name of Automobile Association Developments Limited, whose registered office is Norfolk House, Priestley Road, Basingstoke, Hampshire, RG24 9NY. Registered number 1878835).

Colour separation by Daylight Colour Art Pte Ltd, Singapore
Printed and bound by Dai Nippon Printing Co. (Hong Kong) Ltd.

Acknowledgements
Teresa Fisher wishes to thank the Netherlands Board of Tourism, the VVV, British Midland, KLM uk, Hotel Maas, Hotel Nova, Damstraat Rent-a-Bike and Bikes-a-Gogo for their assistance in preparing this book.
The Automobile Association wishes to thank the following photographers, libraries and museums for their assistance in the preparation of this book: Anne Frankhuis 31a; Mary Evans Picture Library 38b; Museum het Rembrandthuis 44a, 44b; Museum Willet-Holthuysen 42; Eddy Posthuma de Boer 31b, 39, 46; Rex Features Ltd 12; Rijksmuseum Foundation 28a, 28b; Spectrum Colour Library 13a, 19, 20, 45; Van Gogh Museum 26a, 26b; Wyn Voysey 1, 61b; Zefa Pictures 6, 8, 50, 51. The remaining photographs were taken by Ken Patterson and are in the Automobile Association's own Picture Library. Cover: main picture and inset (a) Ken Patterson; inset (b) Image Bank.

SECOND EDITION REVISED BY *George McDonald*

Titles in the CityPack series